Praise for *The Yazoo Pass Expedition: A Union Thrust into the Delta*

The old saw "Come Hell or high water!" could be aptly applied to the Yazoo Pass Expedition in February–April 1863. The Mississippi Delta between Helena, Arkansas, and just north of Vicksburg would be the focus of General Grant's seventh attempt to get into Vicksburg. The "Hell" was the ten-boat flotilla of ironclads and tinclads, with some twenty troop transports carrying several thousand Federal troops to assault and capture Greenwood, Mississippi, and then move into Vicksburg from the northeast. The "high water" was just that—when the levee was blown to flood the area south of Moon Lake and make it possible to send that ominous fleet down the Tallahatchie, Cold Water and Yalobusha Rivers to get to the Yazoo and then Vicksburg via Snyder's Bluff.

Larry McCluney has taken an intense look at this ill-fated expedition and lifted up an unfairly little-known, but extremely important, action for our attention. He has shed light on what was, arguably, one of the most important efforts General Grant made to capture Vicksburg.

The components of high history are all here. The *Star of the West*, the ship that received the first shot of the Civil War, was sunk in the Yazoo to block Federal boats should Fort Pemberton fall; a hastily built cotton bale and dirt earthwork fort sitting on the low bank only a few feet above the water in the river; and a battery of only eight guns in the fort, yet they stopped the Federal fleet and "handled them roughly" in doing so. It is a story of David and Goliath.

The story is well written and takes the reader along at a page-turning clip to see what happens on those bayous and rivers with hard-to-pronounce names down in the delta of Mississippi at a time when the outcome of the campaign—and indeed the war—was much in doubt.

Reading this is time well spent, indeed!

—Dr. Curt Fields, Living Civil War Historian who portrays General Ulysses S. Grant

The Yazoo Pass Expedition

A Union Thrust into the Delta

Larry Allen McCluney Jr.

The History Press

Published by The History Press
Charleston, SC
www.historypress.net

First published 2017

Manufactured in the United States

ISBN 9781625858399

Library of Congress Control Number: 2016956920

This book is dedicated to my great-great-great-grandfather Private John Wesley McCluney, Company F, 3rd Battalion, Mississippi State Troops. Paroled at Vicksburg on July 4, 1863, he later rode with Company F, Mississippi Cavalry, "Forrest's Cavalry."

Contents

PREFACE

The Yazoo Pass Campaign was a joint operation of Major General Ulysses S. Grant's Army of the Tennessee and Rear Admiral David D. Porter's Mississippi River Squadron in the Vicksburg Campaign of the War Between the States. Grant's objective was to get his troops into a flanking position against the Confederate garrison at Vicksburg. The expedition was an effort to bypass the Confederate defenses on the bluffs near the city by using the backwaters of the Mississippi Delta as a route from the Mississippi River to the Yazoo River. Once on the Yazoo, the army would be able to cross the river unopposed and thus achieve its goal. The operation would require a deep penetration into enemy territory that was dominated by water, so cooperation between the two services was necessary. The army was led by Brigadier General Leonard F. Ross. The naval commander was Lieutenant Commander Watson Smith, who was in extremely poor health—this would become an important factor in the expedition's ultimate failure.

The expedition began on February 3, 1863, with the breaching of a levee on the Mississippi River, allowing water to flow from the river into a former channel that connected with the Yazoo River through a series of other waterways. The attacking fleet passed through the cut into Moon Lake, through the Yazoo Pass to the Coldwater River and then into the Tallahatchie, which combines with the Yalobusha to form the Yazoo River, which met the Mississippi a short distance above Vicksburg. From the start, the expedition was delayed by natural obstacles that were more serious than the Confederate resistance, so the armies achieved as little as ten miles (sixteen kilometers) per day. Because progress was so slow, the Confederate army under Lieutenant General John C. Pemberton was able to set up a fort and block passage of the Federal fleet by sinking the *Star of the West* near the town of Greenwood, Mississippi. The Federal fleet did not approach the fort until March 11; then, the ironclad gunboats of the fleet were repulsed in a series of gunfire exchanges on three separate days. The army troops present could not contribute significantly to the battle because of the nature of the ground, much of which was under water.

Following the third repulse on March 16, Lieutenant Commander Smith's health failed him completely, and he turned command over to Lieutenant Commander James P. Foster. Foster and Ross decided to withdraw back to the Mississippi River. Upon reaching the river, they were temporarily persuaded to try again when they met reinforcements for the army, but they resumed their retreat when the new army commander, Brigadier General Isaac F. Quinby, saw the futility of further attacks. The entire force had returned by April 12, and the campaign was over.

The following pages represent an attempt both to bring to life the history of a little-known campaign that gave Vicksburg several more months of preparation before Grant would eventually lay siege to it and to explain how a famous ship known as the *Star of the West* met its fate on the Tallahatchie River just outside Greenwood, Mississippi.

Key to Abbreviations

CWH	Civil War History
CWTI	*Civil War Times Illustrated*
CV	*Confederate Veteran*
HW	*Harper's Weekly*
LOC	Library of Congress
NA	National Archives
NPS	National Park Service
OR	*The War of the Rebellion: A Compilation of the Official Records of the Union and Confederate Armies*
ORN	*Official Records of the Union and Confederate Navies in the War of the Rebellion*
WCNB	Wilson's Creek National Battlefield

Acknowledgements

I am indebted to several people for providing invaluable assistance in the completion of this project. I would like to express my gratitude to Henry McCabe, local historian in Greenwood, Mississippi, who has spent a lifetime of study on the Yazoo Pass Campaign and Fort Pemberton. After years of tours of the fort and papers on its history that he passed on, his pushing of me to write this story was critical. If not for the inspiration from Henry, this project never would have gotten off the ground.

I thank Dr. Curt Fields (aka General Grant) for his support as a fellow living historian, his sustaining encouragement and, above all, his insight and sense of perspective regarding this project. To quote Dr. Fields, "We as living historians are to remember, respect and revere the deeds of these men who fought because they gave their all for a cause they believed was worth fighting and dying for."

I also owe a debt of gratitude to George Conor Bond for his friendly encouragement, careful criticism and friendship as an SCV brother. I want to thank Joe Nokes for helping during those late-night sessions when I could not figure out how the index and endnote programs worked on my computer. Thanks Joe—that's how we roll!

I also want to express my appreciation to the Department of History at Mississippi State University for giving me the opportunity to realize my full potential as a historian. A special thanks goes to Dr. William Parrish for believing in me all those years ago and encouraging me to complete this work.

Finally, a very special expression of appreciation is extended to my parents, Mary and Larry McCluney Sr. (the original Larry), and my loving wife, Julia Annette McCluney, for their support, love and encouragement. "I love you to the moon, the stars and back."

Chapter 1

The Unlucky Ship

The people of Charleston pride themselves upon their hospitality, but it exceeds my expectations. They gave us several balls before we landed.
–Charleston Post and Courier, *"Charleston at War: The Star of the West Gets First Taste of the War," January 2, 2011*[1]

Cornelius Vanderbilt, owner of the *Star of the West*, the pride of Vanderbilt's Atlantic fleet, which carried passengers between New York and Nicaragua. *Courtesy the National Archives.*

The *Star of the West* was running slow in the dark, trying to feel its way into the channel and showing no lights, making it invisible to friend or foe. The ship had arrived outside Charleston Harbor, South Carolina, about 1:30 a.m. The crew was mildly surprised to discover that there were no navigational lights in the city's harbor. The darkness, coupled with the haze, made it nearly impossible to see the target, even though it was only

The USS *Star of the West* approaching Fort Sumter. *Courtesy the Library of Congress.*

a few miles away. Thus, the ship's captain, John McGowan, decided to wait until dawn to bring the vessel in.

For most of the night, the ship crept forward, with the crew on deck taking constant soundings. Most times they measured the same depth: 4.5 fathoms, or about 27 feet. It appeared that they were on the right course.[2]

The ship was originally launched by Jeremiah Simonson on June 17, 1852, as the 1,172-ton civilian brigantine rigged side-wheel steamer SS *San Juan*, later renamed the *Star of the West*. It was built for Cornelius Vanderbilt in Greenpoint, New York, for $250,000. Its length was 228.3 feet and its beam 32.7 feet, with wooden-hull side-paddle wheels and two masts. Its keel was said to be "fashioned out of copper, her hull of white oak, and her interior was sculpted from mahogany." The vessel was the pride of Vanderbilt's Atlantic fleet, which carried passengers between New York and Nicaragua. Then, in 1857, it was purchased by the U.S. Mail Steamship Company; by 1859, it was mainly used in delivery runs between New Orleans and Havana, Cuba, until it was chartered by the U.S. War Department in January 1861.[3]

Following the election of Abraham Lincoln in November 1860, a sectional crisis that had been simmering for at least a decade was triggered. Outraged by the election of a candidate who was known to be opposed to the spread of slavery into new states and territories, leaders of the southern states began to take action to split from the United States. Some prominent southern leaders, Jefferson Davis among them, wanted to give the Lincoln administration a chance to soothe the sectional strife the nation was experiencing. However, the state of South Carolina, which had been asserting its right to secede from the Union for decades, from the time of the Nullification Crisis, was a hotbed of secessionist sentiment. One of its senators, James Chesnut, resigned from

Above: Political cartoon stirring the secession crisis between South Carolina and Washington, D.C. *Courtesy the Library of Congress.*

Right: James Chesnut, a former senator of South Carolina who resigned while supporting the secession of his home state. *Courtesy the Library of Congress.*

Robert Rhett, a former senator of South Carolina who resigned while supporting the secession of his home state and a "fire-eater" who passed the Ordinance of Secession for South Carolina. *Courtesy the National Archives.*

the U.S. Senate on November 10, 1860, only four days after Lincoln's election. His state's other senator resigned the next day. South Carolina would eventually call for a special convention, attended by Robert Rhett and other noted "fire-eaters," and unanimously pass an Ordinance of Secession on December 20, 1860, demanding the immediate withdrawal of Federal troops from within its borders.[4]

In Washington, President James Buchanan, who had been miserable during his time in the White House and couldn't wait to leave office, was thrown into a horrendous situation. In the 1800s, newly elected presidents were not sworn into office until March 4 of the following year, and that meant Buchanan had to spend four months presiding over a nation that was splitting apart.

Meanwhile, in Charleston, South Carolina, Federal troops were commanded by Major Robert Anderson, a proslaver from Kentucky who

President James Buchanan, fifteenth president of the United States, ordered the *Star of the West* to transport troops to Fort Sumter in January 1861. *Courtesy the National Archives.*

remained loyal to the Union. He moved his small garrison of troops from Fort Moultrie, an indefensible spot, to the more modern and more defensible Fort Sumter, in the middle of the harbor. Many South Carolinians cried betrayal, while many Northerners celebrated this show of defiance to Southern secession. By January 1861, tempers were fueling the rumors and flames of war. President Buchanan found himself in a dilemma in which, he fully recognized, making the wrong decision could plunge this country into civil war. Anderson had hastily transferred his troops from Fort Moultrie to Fort Sumter in the middle of Charleston Harbor after South Carolina had passed the Ordinance of Secession in December 1860. Anderson would need supplies to hold his position. Thus, commanding general Winfield Scott picked the USS *Brooklyn*, a naval sloop, to carry men and material to the beleaguered fort. The ship was loaded with about two hundred men, arms, munitions and supplies.

Upon receiving word that the Rebels had scuttled ships in the harbor to make the approach to the fort more difficult, it was decided that an unarmed merchant ship carrying supplies and men could slip into the harbor, make its delivery to the fort and steam away unharmed. With misgivings, President Buchanan approved the chartering of the *Star of the West* at a price of $1,500 per day to carry two hundred soldiers and supplies to Fort Sumter. Captain David Farragut, in command of the *Brooklyn*, was ordered to follow the *Star of the West* in case of an incident. John McGowan, captain of the *Star of the West*, gave this account:

Major Robert Anderson, later promoted to general, commanded the garrison at Fort Sumter, where the first shots of the war were fired. *Courtesy the National Archives.*

Federal troops at Fort Moultrie. *Courtesy of* Harper's Weekly.

After leaving the wharf (from New York) on the 5th inst., at 5 o'clock P.M., we preceded [sic] *down the Bay, where we hove to, and took on board four officers*

General Winfield Scott, known as "Old Fuss and Feathers" and the "Grand Old Man of the Army," served on active duty as a general longer than any other person in American history. Over the course of his fifty-three-year career, he commanded forces in the War of 1812, the Black Hawk War, the Mexican-American War, the Second Seminole War and, briefly, the American Civil War, conceiving the Union strategy known as the Anaconda Plan, which would be used to defeat the Confederacy. *Courtesy the Library of Congress.*

and two hundred soldiers, with their arms, ammunition, &c., and then proceeded to sea, crossing the bar at Sandy Hook at 9 P.M. Nothing unusual took place during the passage, which was a pleasant one for this season of the year.[5]

The mission to bring relief to Fort Sumter was to be a secret mission, but word had gotten back to South Carolina before the *Star of the West* even had a full head of steam in leaving New York Harbor on January 5, 1861. Unfortunately, just about everybody in the government knew of the deception, including Texas senator Louis Wigfall and Secretary of Interior Jacob Thompson of Mississippi. It seems that Thompson resigned his position to return home, but before he did, he sent a telegram to South Carolina governor Francis Pickens about the *Star of the West*. At the same time, the official notification of the mission to Anderson at Sumter was trusted to the regular mails. Pickens immediately warned the Charleston Harbor defenses, and the stage was set. After the *Star of the West* was en route, Secretary of War Joseph Holt received a dispatch from Anderson saying that the garrison was safe and supplies were not needed immediately. Anderson added that the secessionists were building gun emplacements overlooking the main shipping channel into Charleston Harbor. Holt realized that the ship was in great danger and that a war might erupt. He tried in vain to recall the *Star of the West*; Anderson was not aware that the ship continued on its way.[6]

Left: Texas senator Louis Wigfall warned South Carolina governor F.W. Pickens by telegraph of Buchanan's plan to send the *Star of the West* just as he resigned from the Senate. *Courtesy the Library of Congress.*

Right: Secretary of Interior Jacob Thompson of Mississippi. Upon resigning office, he warned South Carolina governor Francis Pickens of the use of the *Star of the West* to resupply Fort Sumter. *Courtesy the Library of Congress.*

Captain McGowan hoped that his vessel would pass for a coastal trader. As the first rays of daylight broke over the Atlantic, the ship steered across the bar and entered the harbor. McGowan reported:

> *We arrived at Charleston Bar at 1:30 A.M. on the 9th inst., but could find no guiding marks for the Bar, as the lights were all out. We proceeded with caution, running very slow and sounding, until about 4 A.M., being then in 4 1/2 fathoms water, when we discovered a light through the haze which at that time covered the horizon. Concluding that the lights were on Fort Sumter, after getting the bearings of it, we steered to the S.W. for the main ship-channel, where we hove to, to await daylight, our lights having all been put out since 12 o'clock, to avoid being seen.*
>
> *As the day began to break, we discovered a steamer just in shore of us, who, as soon as she saw us, burned one blue light and two red lights as signals, and shortly after steamed over the bar and into the ship channel.*

> *The soldiers were now all put below, and no one allowed on deck except our own crew. As soon as there was light enough to see, we crossed the bar and proceeded on up the channel.*[7]

A reporter on board from the *Evening Post* gave this account of what happened next:

> *On we go; the soldiers are below with loaded muskets, and the officers are ready to give the word if there is anything to do. Now it is broad daylight, and we are making directly into the guns of Fort Moultrie, whose black walls are distinctly visible. The little steamer at our right is burning a signal light aft, and is making all possible head-way up the harbor. Now we discover a red Palmetto flag at our left on Morris Island, a little village called Cummings Point, and apparently but little more than a mile from Fort Sumter.*
>
> *"Is it possible that those fellows have got a battery off here?" asks one.*
>
> *"No," answers another, "there is no battery there."*
>
> *But there is. It is now a quarter past seven, and we are about two miles from Forts Sumter and Moultrie, which are equidistant from us, and, suddenly, whiz-z! comes a ricochet shot from Morris Island, and apparently but little more than a mile from Fort Sumter.*
>
> *It plunges into the water and skips along, but falls short of our steamer. The line was forward of our bow, and was, of course, an invitation to stop. But we are not ready to accept the proffered hospitality, and the captain pays no attention to it, except to run up the stars and stripes at the mast-head—a garrison flag which was on board. A moment of anxious suspense, and bang! goes a heavy cannon from the same masked battery. The shot falls short of us a hundred yards or more, and bounds clean over our vessel aft, nearly on a line with the head of a sailor, but luckily a little above it.*
>
> *On we go, and—whizz! again goes the smaller gun first fired, and another ricochet shot skips along the water and falls short of us.*
>
> *"Booh!" exclaims the captain; "you must give us bigger guns than that, boys, or you can not hurt us."*
>
> *On we go, without heeding the compliments of our Charleston friends. Another moment and bang! again goes the heavy gun. The ball now strikes our ship in the fore chains, about two feet above the water. A seaman was holding the lead to take the soundings, and the ball struck directly under his feet. It is not surprising that, under the circumstances, Jack was strongly inclined to take to his heels, and he begins to scramble up with might and*

> *main, when the captain assures him that there is no danger, one ball having struck so near him; on the principle, I suppose, that lightning never strikes twice in the same place. Jack, reassured, patiently takes his place and drops the lead again.*
>
> *The ball, fortunately, was too far spent to go through the side of our vessel, although it left an honorable scar. The battery continues to play upon us, and a huge ball comes clean over us, near the wheel-house. We are not yet within range of the guns of Fort Moultrie, and yonder is a cutter in tow of a steamboat, preparing to open fire upon us. A moment longer and we shall be in range of these three batteries. The gunners on Morris Island are growing confident; if they get the right range they will send a shot through our side, scattering death and destruction. Moultrie, directly in front, will bring her heavy guns to bear, and will drive their deadly missiles into our bow, while the cutter will open on our right.*
>
> *Why does not Major Anderson open fire upon that battery and save us? We look in vain for help; the American flag flies from Fort Sumter, and the American flag at our bow and stern is fired upon, yet there is not the slightest recognition of our presence from the fort from which we look for protection. The unexpected battery on Morris Island has cut off all hope of escape by running the vessel aground near Sumter and taking to the boats. Is it possible that Fort Sumter has been taken by the South Carolinians? If it has not, why does not Major Anderson show that he will protect us, or at least recognize us in some way? To go within range of the guns of Fort Moultrie is to expose vessel, men, and stores to almost instant destruction, or to capture by the enemy.*[8]

As Major Anderson watched the spectacle unfold, he was puzzled by the ship's intentions, as he had received no word of its mission, but there were no doubts as to its purpose near the Charleston Harbor shore batteries. The sentries on Morris Island had spotted the ship just after reveille. The guards had not been overly surprised, as they had been expecting the ship. Years of pent-up Southern frustration were being unleashed on this unlucky ship, for the cadets on Morris Island would not allow it to pass.

There were nearly three hundred troops on the island that morning. Most of them were from local rifle regiments, although forty were cadets from The Citadel. The cadets flew as their banner a unique flag, observed by eyewitnesses on the Federal steamer and described in a dispatch by a Union officer at Fort Sumter as "a flag with a red field, and a white palmetto tree." Just after 7:00 a.m., Major P.F. Stephens ordered the cadets

Artist's rendition based on eyewitness accounts of The Citadel cadets firing on the *Star of the West* from Morris Island. Note the black man assisting the cadets at the cannonballs. *From* Harper's Weekly, *January 26, 1861.*

to fire a shot across the ship's bow, a warning that it should turn around. The cadet who pulled the lanyard was G.E. Haynsworth, and he would go down in local history as the man who fired the first shot of the war.[9]

The troops waited several minutes for a reaction from the *Star of the West.* They were patient, realizing that it could take some time to turn a ship of its size. But the *Star of the West* never deviated from its course. Instead, it kept trudging forward. Stephens watched for any sign of retreat but spotted an entirely unexpected reaction: men on the ship's foremast hoisting a United States flag. Given the circumstances, it was not the reaction Stephens had expected; it also did not have the intended effect. Stevens gave the order to open fire. Cadet Samuel Pickens fired a shot that struck the ship but did little damage. Cadet Thomas Ferguson fired a shot, striking the ship, and another that fell just astern. Altogether, the cadet battery on Morris Island fired seventeen rounds at the *Star of the West*, with three rounds recorded as striking the ship.[10]

Captain McGowan had little working in his favor: he was outgunned, outflanked and quickly running out of water. When the firing began, the *Star of the West* continued to chug through the channel because McGowan felt he didn't have any other choice. If he stopped, the ship could drift and run aground in the outgoing tide. And getting stuck within firing range of Morris Island would have been a death sentence. The captain gave no thought of fighting. The ship was unarmed, and even if McGowan had guns, he was not about to start a war by returning fire. Still, he would not give up easily. He meant to reach Fort Sumter. But soon he realized that he had more problems than a Morris Island battery: ahead, McGowan spotted "a steamer approaching us with an armed schooner in tow." He assumed that the ships meant to intercept him. While he was distracted by the warship off his bow, Fort Moultrie opened fire.[11]

The firing from Morris Island had alerted the troops at Moultrie that something was amiss, and they quickly sprang into action. They, too, had heard the rumors and understood the consequences of allowing the *Star of the West* to reach Sumter. The ship was an easy mark for Moultrie. To reach Fort Sumter, the *Star of the West* had to sail within one mile of the fort. But it wasn't that simple—there were other considerations. If Sumter decided to defend the ship, Fort Moultrie would be facing the full might of a superior fort. It was a dangerous predicament. Ultimately, the state troops at Moultrie decided to open fire, no matter the ramifications. It turned out to be a short engagement. Based on later reports, two shots from Fort Moultrie quickly hit the *Star of the West*, prompting McGowan to give the order to turn around. The *Charleston Mercury* would recount the incident for more than a week, filling the hearts of Charlestonians with pride and admiration for their force of arms.[12]

Between the crossfire and the outgoing tide, it took more than an hour to get the ship clear of the bar. McGowan gave an account of what happened next:

> *At some time there was a movement of two steamers from near Fort Moultrie, one of them towing a schooner (I presume an armed schooner), with the intention of cutting us off. Our position now became rather critical, as we had to approach Fort Moultrie to within three-quarters of a mile before we could keep away for Fort Sumter. A steamer approaching us with an armed schooner in tow, and the battery on the island firing at us all the time, and having no cannon to defend ourselves from the attack of the vessels, we concluded that, to avoid certain capture, or destruction, we would endeavor to get to sea. Consequently we wheeled around and steered down the channel, the battery firing upon us until the shot fell short. As it was now strong ebb tide, and the water having fallen some three feet,*

> *we proceeded with caution, and crossed the bar safely at 8:50 A.M., and continued on our course for this port, where we arrived this morning after a boisterous passage. A steamer from Charleston followed us for about three hours, watching our movements.*[13]

The steamer broke off its pursuit of the *Star of the West* when it finally rendezvoused with its military escort ship, thus easing the nerves of Captain McGowan, who immediately sailed north for New York. The firing on an unarmed ship had been an overt act of war, the Northern papers opined, but the *Star of the West* crew could joke about it by the time they reached New York. "The people of Charleston pride themselves upon their hospitality," one of the officers told the *New York Evening Post*, "but it exceeds my expectations. They gave us several balls before we landed." McGowan praised his crew by saying, "In justice to the officers and crews of each department of the ship, I must add that their behavior while under the fire of the battery reflected great credit on them."[14]

Unfortunately, the *Star of the West* arrived in Charleston at a time when locals were spoiling for a fight. Since the new year began, the city had been on edge, in part because of the news out of Washington. The *Charleston Mercury* reported that U.S. Secretary of War John B. Floyd recommended the federal government abandon Sumter to "prevent civil war." But President Buchanan appeared disinclined to even consider such a notion. The president also did not show any interest in negotiating with Robert Barnwell Rhett, who had been sent to Washington to secure title to all U.S. property in the state, including lighthouses and forts. The *Mercury* kept the city informed of Rhett's progress, or the lack thereof, and suggested that Buchanan's refusal to surrender Sumter constituted a "cause of war."[15]

Little more than an hour after the *Star of the West* made its getaway, a small boat flying a white flag sailed from Sumter toward downtown Charleston. The man in the boat carried a letter from Major Robert Anderson that was addressed to the South Carolina governor. The Fort Sumter commander wanted clarification about the morning's events. The communication from Major Anderson was as follows:

> *To Governor Pickens*
> *To His Excellency the Governor of South Carolina:*
>
> *Sir—Two of your batteries fired this morning on an unarmed vessel bearing the flag of my government. As I have not been notified that war has*

been declared by South Carolina against the United States, I cannot but think this a hostile act, committed without your sanction from opening fire on your batteries. I have the honor, therefore, respectfully to ask whether the above-mentioned act—one which I believe without parallel in the history of our country or any other civilized government—was committed in obedience to your instructions, and notify you, if it is not disclaimed, that I regard it as an act of war, and I shall not, after reasonable time for the return of my messenger, permit any vessel to pass within the range of the guns of my fort.

In order to save, as far as it is in my power, the shedding of blood, I beg you will take due notification of my decision for the good of all concerned. Hoping, however, your answer may justify a further continuance of forbearance on my part, I remain, respectfully,

Robert Anderson.

This was the response of Governor Pickens's office to Major Anderson:

Governor Pickens, after stating the position of South Carolina to the United States, says that any attempt to send United States troops into Charleston harbor to reinforce the fort would be regarded as an act of hostility, and in conclusion adds that any attempt to reinforce the troops at Fort Sumter, or to retake and resume possession of the forts within the waters of South Carolina, which Major Anderson abandoned after spiking the cannon and doing other damages, cannot be regarded by the authorities of the State as indicative of any other purpose than the coercion of the State by the armed force of the Government.

Special agents, therefore, have been off the bar to warn approaching vessels, armed and unarmed, having troops to reinforce Fort Sumter aboard, not to enter the harbor. Special orders have been given the commanders at the forts not to fire on such vessels until a shot across their bows should warn them of the prohibition of the State. Under these circumstances the Star of the West, it is understood, this morning attempted to enter the harbor with troops, after having been notified she could not enter, and consequently she was fired into. The act is perfectly justified by me.

In regard to your threat about vessels in the harbor, it is only necessary for me to say you must be the judge of your responsibility. Your position in the harbor has been tolerated by the authorities of the State, and while the act of which you complain is in perfect consistency with the rights and duties of the State, it is not perceived how far the conduct you propose to adopt can find a parallel in the history of any country, or be reconciled with any other purpose than that of your government imposing on the State the condition of a conquered province.

F.W. Pickens.

In turn, Anderson's response was as follows:

To His Excellency Governor Pickens:

Sir—I have the honor to acknowledge the receipt of your communication, and say that, under the circumstances, I have deemed it proper to refer the whole matter to my Government, and intend deferring the course I indicated in my note this morning until the arrival from Washington of such instructions as I may receive.

I have the honor also to express the hope that no obstructions will be placed in the way, and that you will do me the favor of giving every facility for the departure and return of the bearer, Lieutenant T. Talbot, who is directed to make the journey.

Robert Anderson.[16]

Governor Francis Pickens, no doubt discouraged by Rhett's lack of success in Washington, was condescending in his reply. His letter, reprinted in the *Mercury*, suggested that Anderson had not been "fully informed by your government of the precise relations between it and the State of South Carolina."

Pickens said that Buchanan had received a copy of the Ordinance of Secession and should understand that "sending any reinforcement of troops of the United States in the harbor of Charleston would be regarded by the constitutional authorities of the State of South Carolina, as an act of hostility." Anderson had made it clear that he would not hesitate to fire on South Carolina if provoked, and Pickens had assured him that the state was no friend of the United States government.[17]

On January 12, a *Mercury* headline reported that "Alabama Is Out of the Union." Two days later, word reached Charleston that Florida had also seceded. In fact, Mississippi had been the second state to secede, doing so on January 9 just hours after the *Star of the West* incident. By the end of the month, Georgia, Louisiana and Texas had followed suit, bringing the number

Jefferson Davis, president of the Confederate States of America. *Courtesy the National Archives.*

of states that had seceded to seven. That following February, political leaders of those states agreed to meet in Montgomery, Alabama, in convention with the purpose of creating a Confederate government for those states that had seceded. One week into the convention, the delegates adopted a provisional constitution, most of which had been copied word for word from the U.S. Constitution, and chose Jefferson Davis of Mississippi as its provisional president.[18]

After returning to New York Harbor, the *Star of the West* was mustered into duty as a troop transport and sent to Indianola, Texas, in April 1861. Once again chartered by the U.S. government, its mission was to remove Federal soldiers from Confederate, Texas, who had been gathering at Matagorda Bay, Texas, to New York. On April 16, 1861, Colonel Earl Van Dorn was given orders to prevent the further evacuation of Federal troops from Texas. After securing 125 men and the steamer *Matagorda*, Van Dorn proceeded to Matagorda Bay on April 18. The Federal transport *Star of the West* lay anchored at the mouth of the bay, about twenty-five miles from Indianola. Stopping at Saluria, located at the northern tip of Matagorda Island, Van Dorn transferred his command to the *General Rusk*. The *General Rusk* had been used by Federal troops at Indianola, and Van Dorn hoped that the presence of the vessel near the *Star of the West* would not arouse suspicion. Fortunately for Van Dorn, the Federal warship *Mohawk*, which had been on duty in Matagorda Bay since March 29, was no longer present to interfere with his attempt to capture the *Star of the West*. The *Mohawk* remained constantly under steam in order to be able to immediately respond to any threat to the passenger steamers in the anchorage. However, the policy quickly depleted the *Mohawk*'s stores of fuel, and the ship had departed to procure additional supplies in Havana.[19]

Approaching the *Star of the West* at sundown, Van Dorn informed the watch of the vessel that the *General Rusk* carried troops for embarkation. D.W. Topham, first officer of the *Star of the West*, gave this firsthand account what happened next:

> *The steamer was lying at anchor, at Indianola, expecting to receive troops on board. On the 17th of April the pilot came on board, and told Capt. Howe that 700 Federal troops were coming on the Fashion and another steamer, and requested that he would be ready to receive them at any hour, day or night, that they might arrive alongside. Shortly after midnight, on the 19th, the steamer Rusk came out, and was hailed by Capt. Howe. The Captain of the Rusk in answer said that he had 320 Federal troops which he wished to put on board. All hands were accordingly called out, and every assistance offered to receive the troops. As soon as they were fairly on board Capt. Howe and his officers were surrounded and informed that the steamer was seized by the authorities of Texas, and that they were prisoners. Caught in this trap, resistance was useless, and Capt. Howe reluctantly gave up his ship. The Texans were armed with Minie rifles and swords, Capt. Smith, of the Rusk, was installed as commander of the Star of the West, Capt. Howe and his officers being put below under a guard. Smith pretended that he was acting under orders from the owners of the Rusk, and of the other steamers of the lines between New-Orleans and Texan ports. All these vessels, however, have been seized by the Governor of Louisiana. The steamer was taken to Galveston, where Capt. Smith resigned the command to Capt. Farewell, of the steamer Mexico, and the Star of the West was started for New-Orleans. The old officers of the vessel were sent below and confined in their rooms the night before she reached the mouth of the Mississippi, and they were kept there under guard. After their arrival at New-Orleans, on the 21st, an officer boarded the steamer, and gave notice that all hands must decide in twenty minutes whether they would join the Southern army, or get ready to go home. No one enlisted. The second officer, second and third assistant-engineers, quartermaster's crew and firemen, 39 in all, left the vessel under guard as prisoners of war, expecting to be sent home at the expense of the C.S.A. Capt. Howe, the first and third officers, the chief engineer and the first assistant-engineer decided to stay by the ship, but they were taken ashore and detained until the 25th. On the fifth they were sent to Mobile with an escort, but instead of going to Montgomery,*

> *as they were desired to do, they took the route via Cincinnati, taking a free par from the authorities. They paid their own passages from Cincinnati to New-York. Their thirty-nine companions were taken to Montgomery, where they are now in jail.*[20]

After he and his men were released on the beach, Captain McGowan asked Van Dorn, "Aren't you going to furnish us a military escort for safety?" as he looked about for any concealed Rebel forces. "Safety, hell," replied Van Dorn. "You just surrendered your ship to three Confederates. We have no forces concealed." McGowan exclaimed to Colonel Van Dorn his displeasure over how he lost of his ship when he said roughly, "A dam scurvy trick." To this Van Dorn replied, "You can consider it the fortunes of war. All things are fair when you play that game."[21]

Capturing the *Star of the West* won Van Dorn much acclaim and eventually led to his promotion to brigadier general. As for the *Star of the West*, it was taken to New Orleans and turned over to the Confederate navy, where it was to be armed with two sixty-eight-pounder cannons and two thirty-two-pounder cannons and renamed the CSS *St. Phillip*. But its fame was too well known, and the new name never stuck. It remained docked in New Orleans as a hospital ship and receiving ship from April 1861 until early 1862. There was a suggestion to convert it into an ironclad, which the Confederate navy surely needed for the defense of New Orleans, but its design made the transformation impossible. While in New Orleans, an attempt was ordered on July 4, 1861, by Lieutenant David D. Porter, commanding the USS *Powhatan*, to burn and sink the *Star of the West* to prevent such a conversion, but the plan failed.[22]

After the fall of New Orleans to Admiral David Farragut on April 29, 1862, the Confederate sub-treasury in New Orleans was placed aboard the *Star of the West* and sailed up the Mississippi River to Vicksburg, Mississippi. From Vicksburg, it was sent to the Confederate Navy Yard, where the *Star of the West* was stripped of its engines and masts to reduce difficulties of navigation on the Mississippi and Yazoo Rivers. After the completion of the ironclad ram CSS *Arkansas* in Yazoo City, Captain Isaac N. Brown was ordered by Major General Earl Van Dorn to scuttle the *Star of the West* in the passage of the Yazoo River after the *Arkansas*'s departure. Brown did not, and instead he found another ship of inferior quality as a substitute for the *Star of the West*. The *Star of the West* would remain inactive in Yazoo City until February 1863, when it was moved to Fort Pemberton, just outside Greenwood, Mississippi, by orders of Major General William W. Loring.

Admiral David Farragut ordered the destruction of the *Star of the West* when his fleet entered New Orleans, but it had escaped with the Confederate Treasury to Yazoo City, Mississippi. *Courtesy the National Archives.*

On the morning of March 11, 1863, the *Star of the West* was scuttled by a detachment of the "Carroll Guards," Company C, 20th Mississippi Infantry, led by Lieutenant A.A. Stoddard of Greenwood. Nearly 250 holes were drilled into its white oak hull and plugged until the order was given to sink it to the bottom of the Tallahatchie River next to Fort Pemberton to prevent Union gunboats from navigating past the guns of the fort. Over the next few days, the hulk of the once proud ship slowed the Union ironclads, making them targets for the big guns of Fort Pemberton.[23]

CHAPTER 2

SETTING THE STAGE

We rely greatly on the sure operation of a complete blockade of the Atlantic and Gulf Ports soon to commence. In connection with such blockade we propose a powerful movement down the Mississippi to the ocean, with a cordon of posts at proper points…the object being to clear out and keep open the great line of communication in connection with the strict blockade of the seaboard, so as to envelop the insurgent States and bring them to terms with less bloodshed than by any other plan.

—Winfield Scott, commanding general, May 3, 1861[24]

After the fall of Fort Sumter, President Lincoln declared a naval blockade of all Confederate ports on April 19, 1861. This executive order was followed by a proposal from commanding general Winfield Scott known as the "Anaconda Plan." The plan called for an encirclement of the Confederacy, to be carried out by a naval blockade of the coastline combined with control of the Ohio and Mississippi Rivers by a fleet of gunboats supported by soldiers. Like the powerful South American snake, the plan would squeeze the Confederacy into submission by attrition, cutting it off from economic and military aid from Europe. Scott believed that this would bring the Rebels to terms with less bloodshed than by any other plan by cutting off Confederate overseas trade, shutting off the vital flow of imported arms and exported cotton.[25]

Scott's plan would take time for the navy to acquire enough ships to make the blockade effective and to train the men for the expedition down the

Abraham Lincoln, sixteenth president of the United States. *Mathew Brady, 1864.*

Mississippi River. But there was a drawback to this plan that concerned Scott: "The impatience of our patriotic and loyal Union friends. They will urge instant and vigorous action, regardless I fear, of the consequences." Scott communicated his ideas to President Lincoln, but word leaked out and Northern press proceeded to ridicule it and its creator. Just as Scott predicted, many fire-breathing editors such as Horace Greeley of the *New York Tribune* expected immediate victory, calling the plan undramatic and slow.[26]

At the time of the Civil War, the Mississippi River was the single most important economic feature of the continent, the very lifeblood of America. Upon the secession of the Southern states, Confederate forces closed the river to navigation, and this threatened to strangle Northern commercial interests. President Abraham Lincoln once told his civilian and military leaders, "See what a lot of land these fellows hold, of which Vicksburg is the key! The war can never be brought to a close until that key is in our pocket.... We can take all the northern ports of the Confederacy, and they can defy us from Vicksburg." Lincoln assured his listeners that "I am acquainted with that region and know what I am talking about, and as valuable as New Orleans will be to us, Vicksburg will be more so."[27] The struggle for Vicksburg lasted more than a year, and when it was over, the struggle for Southern independence would be determined.

The centerpiece of the Vicksburg Campaign was the Mississippi River, just as the great river is the centerpiece of the North American continent. The Mississippi and its tributaries drain more than 1 million square miles of territory in the United States and Canada. These waterways included

Wartime Vicksburg. *Courtesy the Library of Congress.*

twenty thousand miles of navigable water extending from Montana to Pennsylvania and from Minnesota to the Gulf of Mexico, making possible the large-scale settlement of the West. Between 1810 and 1860, the number of whites residing west of the Appalachians swelled from 1 million to 15 million, thanks in large part to the availability of navigable waterways. The black population, mostly slaves, grew from 200,000 to more than 2 million, concentrated along the Mississippi. The rivers of the Mississippi basin provided an economic outlet for corn and hogs raised in Iowa and Ohio, as well as the sugar and cotton grown on the great plantations of Louisiana and Mississippi. By 1860, railroads were beginning to penetrate the region, but access to these western rivers remained vital to the economy of both the Midwest and the Deep South.[28]

Soon after the first shots of war were fired, Northern planners almost immediately began devising strategies to open the river to commerce once again. Scott's plan to starve the Confederacy into submission did not accomplish that goal when it came to the Mississippi River, and it became clear that only by opening that river, not blockading it, could the backbone of the Confederacy be broken.[29] Among the plans was the creating of a flotilla that could traverse the river and its tributaries in support of an advancing U.S. army. All that was needed was someone to lead this army and carry out this plan. Such a man was Ulysses S. Grant. With his October 16, 1862 appointment as commander of the Department of the Tennessee, Grant made immediate plans for a campaign south against Vicksburg, Mississippi.

General Ulysses S. Grant was a successful military leader but a failure at everything else. *From* Appomattox, a Limited Series on the Civil War.

Grant came from humble origins. Born and raised in rural Ohio, he graduated from the United States Military Academy in 1843, served with distinction in the Mexican-American War and married the daughter of a slave-owning Missouri farmer. His career went downhill from there. The tedium of peacetime service and the long separations from his family left him bored, depressed and lonely. He acquired a reputation as a heavy drinker. Finally, he resigned his commission in 1854. Grant tried his hand at farming and real estate, without much success. The outbreak of the Civil War found him working as a clerk in his father's Galena, Illinois leather goods store.[30]

From that point on, Grant's rise to prominence was rapid. He began his Civil War career in June 1861 as a colonel commanding a regiment of Illinois volunteers. From there he rose through progressively larger commands, gaining valuable experience at each level. By February 1862, he was commanding a corps-size force in the capture of Forts Henry and Donelson, which brought him to national prominence and earned him a promotion to the rank of major general and command of the Army of the Tennessee.

Modest, quiet and unpretentious, Grant won the respect of his troops and his superiors alike. President Lincoln was pleased to have a general who was more interested in taking the fight to the enemy than in self-promotion: "What I want, and what the people want, is generals who will fight battles and win victories. Grant has done this and I propose to stand by him." Unlike most of his counterparts, Union or Confederate, Grant always based his plans on what he could do to the enemy, rather than worrying about what his enemy might do to him. This mindset got Grant into trouble on several occasions, most notably at Shiloh in April 1862, when a Confederate army under General Albert Sidney Johnston surprised Grant's army in its camps and nearly drove it into the Tennessee River.

That night of the first day of battle, an unperturbed Grant met with a similarly disheveled General William T. Sherman. Sherman was about to ask Grant about his retreat plans but at the last moment decided against it. Instead, he said, "Well, Grant, we've had the devil's own day, haven't we?" "Yes," the commanding general responded and, after a pause, "lick 'em tomorrow, though." Most generals would have retreated after such a mauling. The next day, Grant counterattacked at dawn and drove the Confederates from the field. More importantly, Grant was one of the first Union generals to recognize the fact that the war could not be won simply by outmaneuvering the enemy or occupying a few vital centers. Shiloh taught Grant that the conflict would not end until the Confederate armies were beaten into submission. He believed in seizing the initiative and never relinquishing it, giving his opponents no opportunity to rest or reconstitute. After Shiloh, Grant was considered a dangerous opponent for any Southern commander.[31]

Confederate general Albert Sydney Johnston was the hope of the Confederacy in the West. He died at the Battle of Shiloh on April 6, 1861. *Courtesy the Library of Congress.*

After the fall of New Orleans on May 2, 1862, Confederate forces began to move quickly to reinforce the vital river port of Vicksburg. Fortifications on the high bluffs of the Yazoo River north of Vicksburg were constructed at Snyder's Bluff in order to secure the Confederate right flank and to control the mouths of the Yazoo and its tributaries, the Great Sunflower and Little Sunflower Rivers. Confederate gun emplacements located at water level and on the bluffs would command the river approaches to Vicksburg, thus allowing the Confederates to control the river traffic to and from the Gulf of Mexico. These new defenses and reinforced river batteries helped secure the Confederate western flank and command the defense of the Mississippi River, its tributaries and bayous against a superior Union navy.[32]

On October 20, Major General John A. McClernand secured command of the short-lived Army of the Mississippi, with the express mission of seizing Vicksburg. A dubious political appointment made by President Lincoln, its effect was soon nullified by political pressure within the Regular Army.[33] Grant proceeded with his own campaign plans, never overtly acknowledging McClernand. Assuming departmental command on October 25, Grant had his troops gathered around La Grange, Tennessee, north of the Mississippi state line, just a few miles west of Grand Junction, Tennessee. By November 5, Grant had begun his first overland push into Mississippi with the goal of capturing Vicksburg. By the fall of 1862, north Mississippi was securely in the hands of the Union army after the Battles of Shiloh, Iuka and

General William T. Sherman was Grant's closest confidant and friend throughout the war. He was known as "Uncle Billy" by his troops. *Mathew Brady.*

Corinth. Grant's first strategy for Vicksburg called for a dual advance with Major General William Tecumseh Sherman. Grant wanted to follow the line of the Mississippi Central Railroad south toward Vicksburg, hoping to stall the Confederate army near Grenada and allow Sherman to take Vicksburg with little resistance—or, if possible, he would push the Confederates to "the gates of Vicksburg." As he moved his army down the main rail line through the heart of Mississippi, capturing the towns and rail along the way, Sherman would provide the second punch, arriving to the north of Vicksburg from Memphis. They, along with the Federal navy, would surround and capture the city, thus dividing the Confederacy and ultimately leading to the restoration of the Union. But gaining Vicksburg would prove much more difficult.[34]

Supplies were to come south from Columbus, Kentucky, by way of the Tennessee & Ohio Railroad and at Grand Junction switch onto the Mississippi Central track for the journey south. All that was needed was approval from Washington, D.C. General-in-Chief Henry W. Halleck gave approval to Grant's plan to "move your troops as you may deem best to accomplish the great objective in view." All the available resources in his department would be at his disposal, as well as all necessary transports in St. Louis, Missouri. Grant asked Rear Admiral David D. Porter to cooperate as well. Once Grant had received authority from Halleck to proceed, he sent a telegram to Sherman. Sherman was to return from Oxford, Mississippi, to Memphis, Tennessee, with one division; assume command of troops being assembled there by

General Henry Halleck, general-in-chief of the Union armies, tried on many occasions to replace General Grant because he believed Grant was an alcoholic and unreliable. He would eventually become Grant's chief of staff when Grant was promoted to lieutenant general. *Courtesy the Library of Congress.*

McClernand; and, with the cooperation of Porter, descend the Mississippi to the mouth of the Yazoo River, north of Vicksburg.

Supported by Porter's gunboats, Sherman was to ascend the Yazoo a short distance, disembark his thirty-two-thousand-man army and "proceed to the reduction of that place" by seizing the high ground northeast of Vicksburg to keep the Vicksburg defenders from being reinforced. If the mission was a success and Vicksburg fell, his soldiers could then form the right wing of Grant's army as he moved down the Mississippi Central Railroad, capturing the vital railroad junction of Jackson, Mississippi.[35]

With little force to oppose him, Grant began his first march to Vicksburg, following the Mississippi Central Railroad out of southwest Tennessee. This generated a frenzy of activity for the Confederate army scattered across north Mississippi. On October 1, 1862, the Confederacy established a new military department that would incorporate the Department of Mississippi and east Louisiana, including both Port Hudson and Vicksburg. Commanding the Confederate forces in Mississippi was the Pennsylvania-born Confederate commander Lieutenant General John C. Pemberton, who found a poorly organized department that relied on Major General Earl Van Dorn's troops, recently defeated at Corinth, and then in action against the Union rear, supplied by Brigadier General Nathan Bedford Forrest. Upon assuming his new command and establishing his headquarters in Jackson, Mississippi, Pemberton found out that he had new responsibilities that included the command of forces operating in southwest Tennessee. Confederate secretary of war George Randolph directed Pemberton that his first priority

Lieutenant General John C. Pemberton, commander of the Army of Mississippi. A Pennsylvanian by birth, he married a Virginian and took up the cause of his newly adopted state. *Courtesy the Library of Congress.*

was the defense of the department and that he was to report directly to the War Department.[36]

Pemberton had in his department approximately 54,050 officers and men who reported present for duty in January 1863. Of these, about 12,375 were in Port Hudson, Louisiana. Another 1,400 were located in Columbus, Mississippi; 21,000 were in Vicksburg; and 19,275 were available spread out on the Mississippi Delta along the Tallahatchie and Yazoo Rivers. All Confederate naval forces on the Mississippi River and its tributaries were organized into the Naval Forces of the West, commanded by Flag Officer W.F. Lynch.[37]

By December 1, Grant's troops were facing Confederates, in shallow trenches, along the Tallahatchie River, north of Oxford, Mississippi, thirty-five miles south of Grand Junction. A large Union supply depot had been established at Holly Springs, Mississippi, a little over fifteen miles north along the Mississippi Central Rail Railroad.

On December 1, resisting Mississippi Confederates, close by the railroad north of Abbeville, pulled out of south-bank entrenchments along the Tallahatchie River and moved south. With Union XIII Corps's cavalry commander Colonel T. Lyle Dickey ordered to pursue, he gathered his troops near Abbeville. A hot skirmish was fought in Oxford on December 2 as the Federal advance encountered the

Colonel T. Lyle Dickey, who was routed by Confederates at Coffeeville, Mississippi. *Courtesy of Find-a-Grave.com.*

Confederate rear guard, led by Van Dorn just north of town. Colonel John K. Mizner of the 3rd Michigan engaged Confederate forces on the hills northwest near the rail line, while the 7th Kansas and 4th Illinois pushed down the main road to the center. The skirmishing continued right to the town square, where the Rebels made a stand before Federal reinforcements were called in and drove them south toward the Yokona River. Fletcher Pomeroy, 7th Kansas Cavalry and now orderly to Colonel Thomas P. Herrick, gave this account of the skirmish:

> *Tuesday, 2nd. Oxford, Miss. Our brigade moved out of camp at 3 A.M. with three days rations, and crossed the Tallahatchie on the main road. The rebel works at that point are very strong, and they might have offered a strong resistance if we had attempted to have taken them by assault. A flank movement by our right wing compelled an evacuation without a battle. We moved on through Abbyville and met the enemy near Oxford about 2 o'clock. Some pretty sharp fighting followed but we succeeded in driving him into, through and beyond the town. Eight rebels were killed and several wounded and captured. I took two prisoners. We had pushed our way along the streets and alleys and across the house lots to within three blocks of the public square, when we were obliged to call for re-enforcements as there was a strong force of the enemy there.*
>
> *While we were waiting for the re-enforcements to come up, Col. Herrick and I were standing just at the edge of the main street. Presently we realized that we were targets for some sharp shooter up the street. We drew back a little and soon saw a man come from behind a building and stand beside a nearby tree and fire and then step back. I trained my carbine on that spot, and when he appeared again I pulled the trigger before he had a chance to. He jumped back without firing and did not show up again. As we were falling back after having driven the Johnnys through town, I had occasion to stop so got behind. As I hurried on to overtake the command I discovered two rebels crawling out of a corncrib beside the road. I succeeded in "surrounding" them and took them into camp, muskets and all. They evidently thought the coast was clear and that they could safely crawl out and get away. We are camped in the town tonight. It is a fine town.*[38]

On December 3, Dickey divided his force in four different parts: first a regiment secured Oxford; Colonel John K. Mizner's men, dispatched west, roved the right flank looking for the Confederates; and Colonels Albert

L. Lee and Edward Hatch headed up two columns, Hatch's traveling the Coffeeville Road south and Lee's moving down a parallel route on the east. Grant sent Dickey encouragement to press the Confederates as far as possible. Hatch hit stout resistance on the Yocknapatalfa River. Following behind his columns, Dickey sent word forward ordering Lee to ride to Hatch's support, cross the river and then press on for Coffeeville.[39]

Dickey caught up with his force the next day below the Yocknapatalfa at Water Valley, Mississippi, and found that rough terrain and resistance had kept Lee and Hatch from receiving orders. They met at Water Valley by accident after Hatch was driven from the hamlet by superior numbers. At Dickey's direction, Mizner also arrived shortly.

Union units, with some scattered below the Confederates at Grenada and others to the west, composed the nearest support. Dickey, unsure of Confederate numbers behind or in front, decided to press pursuit one more day, perhaps making contact with other Union forces.

Dickey's men crossed the Otuckalofa River south of Water Valley the morning of the December 5, pressing down the Coffeeville Road as one column. They hit Van Dorn's skirmishers at 2:00 p.m. and fanned out, forming a broad front; they moved within a mile of Coffeeville. Resistance briefly cooled. Having hauled two cannons with them, they probed the Confederates' front with artillery fire. Major General Mansfield Lovell and Brigadier General Lloyd Tilghman, Van Dorn's subordinates, commanded the defense. From a screened front, Confederates answered with six cannons and sent an infantry battle line forward. Benjamin Dill and John R. McClanahan, owners of the *Memphis Appeal*, being printed in Grenada after the fall of Memphis, gave this account:

> *Compelled to turn at bay by the slowness with which the trains were moved, parts of General Tilghman's and Rust's divisions formed in the line of battle on the hills three quarters of a mile north of Coffeeville, and with the cavalry and six pieces of artillery in the center, quietly awaited the onset of the enemy, who were slowly driving in a small party of our sharpshooters, which had been bravely skirmishing with him for more than an hour from one to two miles in front.*[40]

Union troops, reeling under superior fire, organized a fighting retreat and withdrew, alternating defensive lines. Tilghman admitted that "the tactics of the enemy did them great credit" but volunteered pursuit. Colonel William H. Jackson's seven hundred cavalry and about six hundred infantry pressed

General Joseph E. Johnston, commander of the Confederate Department of the West. *Courtesy the Library of Congress.*

Dickey's force until nightfall, when the Federals secured a superior position opposite a large open field. The engagement broke off.[41]

Pemberton had to rely on General Joseph E. Johnston for supervision in the defense of Vicksburg. Johnston had been given this task on November 24, but little advice had been forthcoming. When Pemberton requested aid from General Braxton Bragg in Tennessee, Bragg told Pemberton that he was preparing for his Murfreesboro Campaign (which would end in the Battle of Stones River) and could offer no material assistance, but he could order Forrest's cavalry to hit Grant's supply lines. This was Forrest's Second Raid.

Beginning on December 11, Forrest destroyed great portions of Tennessee rail line and threatened Grant's Columbus, Kentucky railhead, forcing Grant to switch his base of supply to Memphis, Tennessee. He then sent his materials east on the Memphis & Charleston Railroad to Grand Junction. However, on December 20, Van Dorn led 3,500 cavalry from Grenada, south of Grant's lines, and attacked the Union general's Holly Springs supply base. The Holly Springs Raid resulted in the loss of more than $1.5 million in Union supplies. Colonel Benjamin H. Grierson pursued Van Dorn in vain for days before the Confederates easily reentered Southern lines at Grenada.[42]

Grant realized the error of trying to maintain his supply and communication lines along rail lines, and within a week of the Holly Springs Raid, he had withdrawn most of his forces to La Grange. Sherman was unaware that Grant was withdrawing from his North Mississippi Central Railroad Campaign and proceeded with his part of the plan. On December 26, Sherman's transports entered the Yazoo River, and before nightfall, three divisions had landed at

Johnson's Plantation. Confederate reinforcements had already arrived. The officer in direct command of the defenses of Vicksburg was Major General Carter L. Stevenson, who commanded four brigades led by Brigadier General Seth M. Barton, John C. Vaughn, John Gregg and Edward D. Tracy. Brigadier General Stephen D. Lee commanded a provisional division, with brigades commanded by Colonels William T. Withers and Allen Thomas; Lee was the

Brigadier General Stephen D. Lee. *Courtesy of Donna R Causey.*

primary commander of the Confederate defense in the Walnut Hills[43] until the arrival late on the twenty-ninth of Major General Carter L. Stevenson. Although the Union forces outnumbered the men to their front by 30,720 to 13,792, they faced a formidable natural and man-made defense. First was a thick entanglement of trees, which was broken intermittently by swampland. Chickasaw Bayou—a stream that was chest-deep, fifty yards wide and choked with trees—also acted as a potential barrier to Sherman's men because it was parallel to the planned line of advance and could interrupt communication between units. Furthermore, the Confederates had formed dense barriers using felled trees for abatis.[44]

News that the invasion convoy was approaching the Yazoo had sent Confederates into the rifle pits covering the approaches to Walnut Hills, also known as Chickasaw Bluffs. As Sherman's men disembarked facing these distant bluffs, Porter's gunboats moved up the river, shelling the

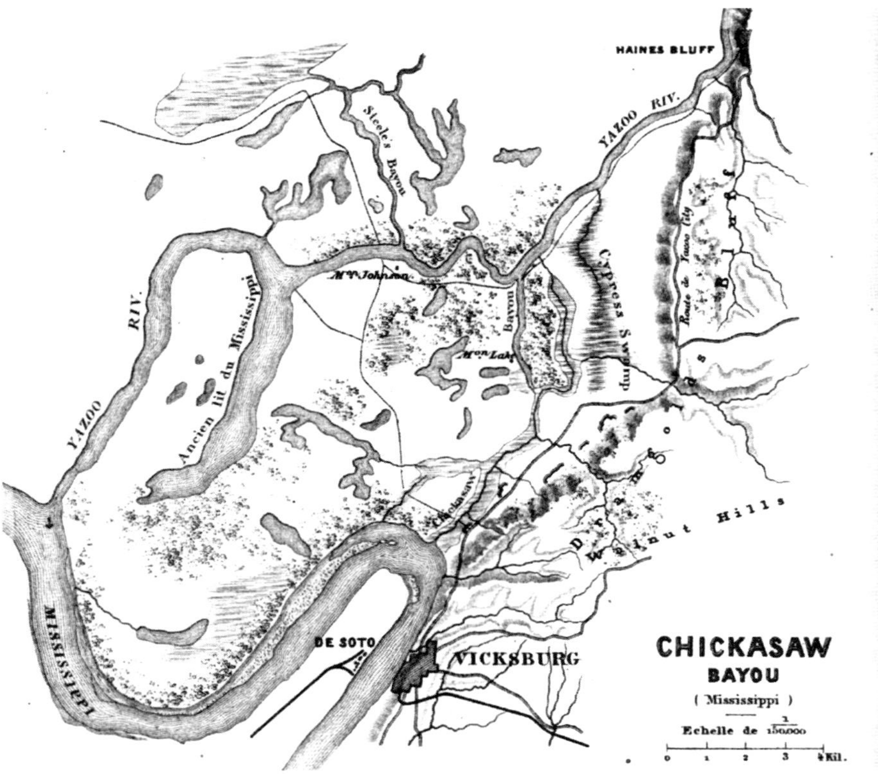

Battle map of General William T. Sherman's failed attempt to approach Vicksburg by capturing Chickasaw Bluffs. *From* Iron Brigader, Civil War Info and Resources.

Chickasaw Bluffs from Union lines. *Courtesy the Library of Congress.*

Chickasaw Bluffs from Union lines. *From* Iron Brigader, Civil War Info and Resources.

Battlefield of Chickasaw Bayou by the photographer William Redish Pywell. It appears to show a wagon, limber or caisson partially submerged in water. Amazingly, there also appears to be the body of a soldier lying in the mud beyond and just above the wagon wheel. If this photo is correctly identified, it may be the only known image of the Chickasaw Bayou battlefield at or near the time of the battle. *Courtesy the Library of Congress.*

Confederate batteries on Haynes' Bluff on the Union left. Union troops deployed on rough ground, with an enormous swamp in the front and the bluffs beyond.

On December 27, after a heavy artillery bombardment of the Confederates, the Federals pressed forward through swampland until they reached water barriers fronting the Confederate defenses. Officers complained that they found only four approaches to the bluffs not barred by water, and those were swept by Confederate artillery.

Brigadier General Frederick Steele's division sought to reach the bluffs on the twenty-eighth, crossing Blake's Levee, but was checked by Confederate abatis and cannons. Sherman decided to assault the center. After a four-hour artillery barrage on the Confederate defenses, at noon on the twenty-ninth two brigades charged across Chickasaw Bayou causeway to the foot of the bluffs and were ravaged by Confederate fire from high ground. The twisted swampland hindered Federals in bringing up artillery support. Confederate positions gave them a clear field of fire. Thrusts to keep the Confederates pinned down were unsuccessful, and Sherman recalled his troops.[45]

That evening, Sherman declared that he was "generally satisfied with the high spirit manifested" by his men, although their attacks had failed in the face of strong Confederate positions on the high bluffs. Federal casualties were 208 killed, 1,005 wounded and 563 captured or missing; Confederate casualties were 63 killed, 134 wounded and 10 missing. Sherman conferred with Porter, whose naval gunfire had also failed to do any significant damage to the enemy. They decided to resume the attacks on the following day, but after being advised that more reinforcements had joined Pemberton from

Bragg's Army of Tennessee, Sherman withdrew his men from the Yazoo on January 2, 1863. At that time, Confederate defenders numbered 14,000. This ended Grant's first Vicksburg Campaign.[46]

Chapter 3

Formulating a Plan

Boldness in execution is nearly always necessary, but in planning and fitting out expeditions or detachments great circumspection is a virtue.
–Lieutenant General Winfield Scott[47]

Van Dorn's raid and the Battle of Chickasaw Bayou produced nothing during the December push against Vicksburg. Grant fell back to Memphis. Sherman was ordered to withdraw the thirty-thousand-man column before the Walnut Hills to the Yazoo River, into the Mississippi River and up that vast and turbulent stream. His forces reunited, Grant—a stubborn, good soldier—studied the problem in his quiet fashion, a cigar between his teeth, looking at a map of the region. His instinct was always to strike out straight before him. The river, for all its windings, was the most direct road to Vicksburg. Late in January 1863, he brought a great army down the Mississippi River and landed it on the Louisiana side, some miles above the town that must be taken. Here, above the line of danger from the Confederate river batteries, he anchored his ships of war. The weather was appalling—cold rain fell for days on end. The Mississippi River was already at flood stage, causing the backwaters to inundate the lowlands of Louisiana, leaving very little high ground for the troops to camp and forcing a large number of troops to be quartered on the transports.[48]

It was sheer misery for the troops. The ground was so saturated that wells and latrines were impossible, so soldiers drank and relieved themselves all along the muddy shores, causing sickness of every description to sweep through the camps. "Some have the chills & a good many the diareah & none of them seem to be in very good spirits," wrote William Winters of the 67th Indiana.

Hundreds of men died within weeks, causing the living and the dead to share the high ground. "The levee for long distances is full of new made graves," reported Cyrus F. Boyd of the 15th Iowa. "This is a hard place for a sick man. He must have plenty of grit or die." Morale was declining, desertions and sickness were increasing and many soldiers were dying from disease, including pneumonia and smallpox.[49]

Until the waters subsided, Grant and his staff pondered how to keep his troops busy until he could begin active campaigning in the spring, so he ordered them to undertake several moves that would give the appearance of activity but would not bring on a major battle. From higher ground and reaches of the river far above Vicksburg, Grant studied his map for flanking movements; the Yazoo seemed a stream of ill omen. Although Grant was not a superstitious man, he did not like retracing his steps. He was a plain, straightforward and not overly imaginative, introspective or sophisticated person; he did not so much plan great campaigns but rather unswervingly believed in taking the next common-sense step in his planning. His merit was that in the all-pervading fog of war, it was usually on firm ground that he set his step. Not always, but usually.

The Yazoo flowed southward from the Tennessee line. There it was called the Coldwater. Farther down, in northern Mississippi, it became the Tallahatchie, into which flowed the Yalobusha. Lower yet it was named the Yazoo, and so flowed into the Mississippi. Throughout its course, it drained a vast, flat lowland, overshot by innumerable lesser streams, lakes and bayous, rising into ridge and bluff at the southern end. Named the Mississippi Delta, it was reported to be an enormous fertile alluvial plain and a storehouse from which Vicksburg and all the Confederate armies in Tennessee and Mississippi were fed. Moreover, at Yazoo City, where the three streams became finally the Yazoo, there existed the Confederate Navy Yard, where gunboats were being built. To get into that region from the northern end, gunboats and troop transports had to come down those rivers, surprise Yazoo City, destroy the navy yard and then move on to take Vicksburg. Grant reached for another cigar and studied the map closer, noticing that the delta had few roads, and although the Yazoo was navigable from Yazoo City downward, the Tallahatchie and the Coldwater were not. Then Admiral David D. Porter came in with a well-considered plan, a joint army-navy expedition.[50]

Admiral David Dixon Porter was the foster brother of Admiral David G. Farragut, who had captured New Orleans and Mobile. Porter would be a great asset to Grant in many campaigns that involved joint naval and army operations. *Courtesy of National Park Service.*

Porter, a Pennsylvanian by birth, was the son of Commodore David Porter, hero of the War of 1812; his half-brother was William D. "Dirty Bill" Porter, and his foster brother was (James) David G. Farragut. At the age of ten, David sailed with his father to the West Indies, and at age thirteen, he joined the Mexican navy as a midshipman. At the age of sixteen, David joined the United States Navy. He later served in the Mediterranean and South Atlantic Squadrons during the Mexican-American War. When the Civil War began, he was promoted to commander and was assigned to take command of the USS *Powhatan*. In March 1862, Commander Porter assisted then captain Farragut's West Gulf Blockading Squadron in the capture of New Orleans. In October 1862, Porter took command of the "Brown Water Navy" on the rivers. He took part in the capture of Fort Hindman in January 1863 and the capture of Vicksburg in July 1863. After Vicksburg, Porter was promoted to rear admiral. From March to May 1864, Porter's fleet had a disastrous experience trying to cooperate with land forces in an attack on Shreveport, Louisiana, during the Red River Campaign. After this fiasco, Porter was transferred to command the North Atlantic Squadron. Once the Civil War ended, he was promoted to vice admiral in 1866 and became the superintendent of the U.S. Naval Academy. He would eventually become admiral under President Grant in 1870.[51]

A civilian pilot, J.F. Morton, suggested to Porter the Yazoo Pass route, located some distance below Memphis. The Yazoo Pass was a point where the Mississippi and the Coldwater came within calling distance of each other. Between was the Yazoo Pass, where a levee had been built years before, shutting off the bayou from river and preventing floods in the region. Porter proposed to assemble a fleet, cut the levee and lift the water in the Coldwater and the Tallahatchie Rivers. The fleet would then proceed down those streams with ironclads and as many transports as needed, take Yazoo City, enter the Yazoo and approach Vicksburg from the north. Grant, writing in his memoirs long after the event, stated that he did not have great confidence that the expedition would prove successful, but there was a whole army of strong young men with nothing to do and it seemed to Grant that they should be working instead of idle. Furthermore, all this activity was to likely confuse the Confederates and keep them from finding out Grant's true plans. If the expedition was a success, he was prepared to take advantage of it.[52]

It occurred to Grant that if the levee were blown, reopening the Yazoo Pass, a joint army-navy expedition could make a roundabout flanking movement through these meandering waterways and reach Haynes' Bluff north of Vicksburg. Grant also saw another potential benefit that the Yazoo Pass route offered: with the spring campaigning season fast approaching, Grant became very concerned about the dwindling forces in the Department of Tennessee and the potential Confederate threat to retake northern Mississippi. Van Dorn's attempt in October 1862 to retake the vital railroad crossing at Corinth, Mississippi, had failed only by a slim margin. Another attempt just might succeed. Grant wanted the Yazoo Pass Expedition to make a side trip to Grenada and burn the railroad bridge, the same bridge that Hovey's raid had failed to burn in December 1862. With the bridge gone, Grant would not have to worry about Pemberton using the Mississippi Central Railroad to make a northern thrust.[53]

With careful consideration of his plan, Grant wrote to Porter the following:

> *I would respectfully advise the following programme to be followed, as near as practicable, by the expedition through Yazoo Pass:*
>
> *They necessarily go through the Pass into Coldwater River, thence down that stream into the Tallahatchie, which, with its junction with the Yalobusha, forms the Yazoo, which it is the great of the expedition to enter.*
>
> *At the town of Marion* [Greenwood], *on the Yazoo River,* [the enemy] *were said at one time to have had a battery, but it has been removed, and, unless a mistrust of our present design has induced the enemy to reoccupy that point, no guns will be found there. It would be well, however, to approach it carefully.*
>
> *Below Marion* [Greenwood] *the river divides, forming a very large island, the right-hand branch, descending, being known as the Big*

> *Sunflower, or at least connecting with it, and the left-hand branch retains the name of Yazoo. On this is Yazoo City, where in all probability steamers will be found; and if any gunboats are being constructed, it is at this place.*
>
> *Accordingly to the information I receive, most of the transports are up the Sunflower River. I would, therefore, advise that both of these streams, and in fact all navigable bayous, be well reconnoitered before the expedition returns. The Yalobusha is a navigable stream to Grenada. At this place the railroad branches, one going to Memphis, the other to Columbus, Ky. These roads cross the river on different bridges. The enemy are now repairing both these roads, and on the upper one, the one leading through the middle of* West *Tennessee, have made considerable progress. I am liable at all times to be compelled to divert from the Mississippi River expedition a large portion of my forces on account of the existence of these roads. If these bridges can be destroyed, it would be a heavy blow to the enemy, and of much service to us. I have directed 600 men, armed with rifles, to go up on transports to Delta, leaving here to-morrow, to act as marines to the expedition. Have also ordered the regiments spoken of this morning to report at steamer Magnolia at 10 a.m. to-morrow, to join your service.*[54]

The western part of the state of Mississippi, from the Tennessee state line on the north and Vicksburg on the south, is a part of the floodplain of the Mississippi River. The region is described as quite low; in many places, it is lower than the level of the river. It is occupied by numerous marshes, canebrakes, sloughs, bayous, lakes, creeks and interconnecting waterways, such as the Coldwater, Sunflower, Tallahatchie, Yalobusha, Yazoo, Yocuna, Bogue Phalia, Steele's Bayou and Deer Creek.[55]

Until the middle of the nineteenth century, overflow from the Mississippi continued to pass into these waters, and they could be used as alternatives to the main river for water transportation. One such route left the Mississippi at a point a little south of Helena, Arkansas, passed through an oxbow lake (a former loop of the river that had been cut off when it changed course) known as Moon Lake and followed the Yazoo Pass to the Coldwater River. The Coldwater is a tributary of the Tallahatchie River; this combines with the Yalobusha to form the Yazoo River at Greenwood, Mississippi.

The Yazoo then flows 188 miles to reenter the Mississippi a short distance above Vicksburg. This changed in 1856, however, when the coming of the railroad induced the state to drain some of the land for agricultural uses. To that end, it built artificial levees to confine the river to its main course.

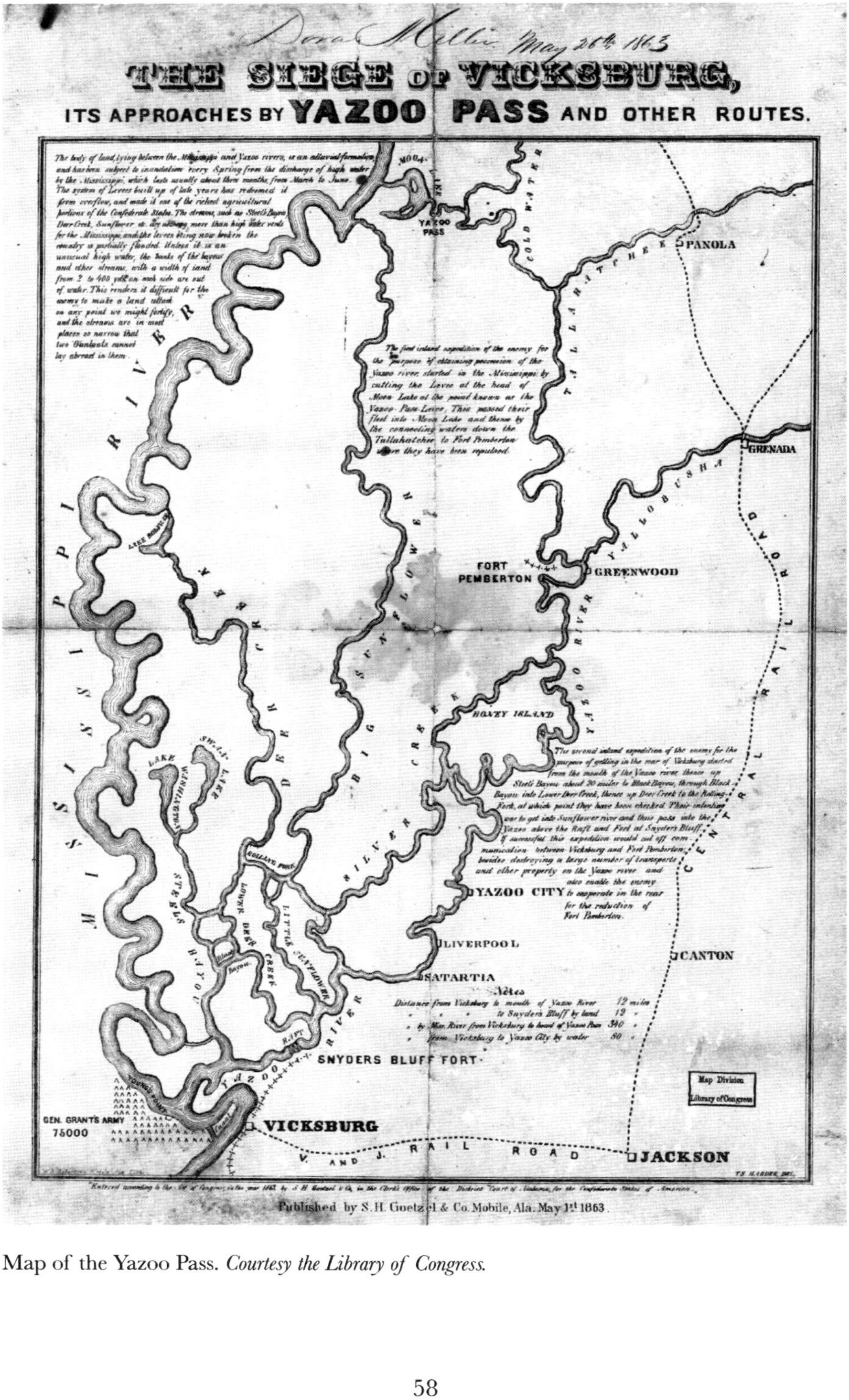

Map of the Yazoo Pass. *Courtesy the Library of Congress.*

This photo was taken after the Vicksburg Campaign of Major General Wilson, who is seated in the chair on the far left. After his success as Grant's chief of engineers, he was promoted and placed in command of Sherman's Cavalry Corps. His cavalry would capture Confederate president Jefferson Davis in Georgia in May 1865. *From the Photographic History of the Civil War.*

Deprived of its principal source, the water level behind the levee dropped as much as eight feet.[56]

To see if the expedition was feasible, on January 29, 1863, Grant sent Lieutenant Colonel James H. Wilson to survey the levee. As he stated in his memoirs:

> *Lieutenant-Colonel Wilson was sent to Helena, Arkansas, to examine and open a way through Moon Lake and the Yazoo Pass if possible. Formerly there was a route by way by inlet from the Mississippi River into Moon Lake, a mile east of the river, thence east through the Yazoo Pass to Coldwater, along the later to the Tallahatchie, which joins the Yalobusha about two hundred and fifty miles below Moon Lake and forms the Yazoo River. These were formerly navigated by steamers trading with the rich plantations along their banks; but the state of Mississippi built a strong levee across the inlet some years ago, leaving the only entrance for vessels into the rich region the one byway of the mouth of the Yazoo several hundreds of miles below.*[57]

On February 2, Wilson wrote to Grant:

> *We reached Helena last night, and had all arrangements complete to start from there this morning at 10 o'clock. General Gorman accompanied me, sending under my command 500 men, provided with two days' rations, and implements complete for the necessary labor. He returned to Helena this evening, and will send down all the provisions, tents needed.*
>
> *I arrived at the levee across the Pass about noon, and found a much more favorable state of affairs than I at first anticipated. The stream looks quite navigable, and I am sure will allow the boats now here to navigate it without difficulty. I had the men at work cutting the embankment by 2 o'clock and by to-morrow night will have a water-way 20 yards wide cut. The difference of level between the water outside and inside of the levee is 8 1/2 feet.*
>
> *The steamers Henderson and Hamilton came in the Pass this afternoon, landed against the embankment, and turned about without difficulty, and went back into the Mississippi.*
>
> *...There are two entrances into the Pass; the lower one is the one formerly used, but the upper is the one through which our boats passed to-day, and is the best. You will also perceive that the levee is a very heavy one, and, therefore, will require a good deal of work to cut through: but from the fact that there is 8 1/2 feet difference of level between the water inside and out, once opened, the crevasse will enlarge very rapidly. The back country both north and south of the pass is partially over flowed by water from crevasses in the levee. I think boats can go through our cut in three days. The undertaking promises fine results.*[58]

Digging began on February 2, 1863, on the eighteen-foot-high, one-hundred-foot-long levee, and the next day, a mine was detonated in the remaining gap between the Mississippi and Moon Lake. Union pioneers blew up the levee with a thunderous explosion on February 3, creating a channel through an opening that was forty yards wide. Grant wrote that this new passageway to Vicksburg would open up new avenues of attack and would "prove a perfect success."[59]

The Yazoo Pass became a furious yellow torrent where the torn arms of trees became abatis in motion. The Coldwater received the flood and bore it on to the Tallahatchie. So angry were the churning waters by the gate in the levee that days passed before the ironclads *Baron De Kalb* and *Chillicothe*; the rams *Fulton* and *Lioness*; the tinclads *Forest Rose*, *Marmora*, *Rattler*, *Romeo*, *Petrel*

USS *Chillicothe* was a City Class ironclad designed by Samuel M. Pook and constructed by the self-taught engineer James Buchanan Eads. The ironclad participated in many important military campaigns during the Civil War, such as the Battle of Belmont, the Battle of Shiloh, the Siege of Island No. 10, the Battle of Memphis, the Siege of Vicksburg and the Tennessee and Cumberland River Expeditions, along with the Yazoo, White and Red River Campaigns. *Courtesy the National Park Service.*

USS *Baron De Kalb*. Originally commissioned the USS *St. Louis*, its name was changed later. It was a City Class ironclad designed by Samuel M. Pook and constructed by James Buchanan Eads. *Courtesy the National Park Service.*

and *Signal*; and all the transports in the rear could attempt that newly made passage. Wilson said the water poured with great velocity, like nothing he had seen before except Niagara Falls. He reported it would take four to five days for the water to settle before they could enter the pass.[50]

On February 7, Wilson boarded the *Forrest Rose*, the expedition's flagship, and went into Moon Lake. They proceeded to the mouth of the Yazoo Pass, where it leaves Moon Lake, and explored the pass. On February 9, Wilson wrote to Grant about his findings:

> *General, I have been waiting all day for a boat to return to Vicksburg, in order to report in person the condition of affairs in Yazoo Pass; but as an expedition has already been arranged, and you gave me permission to accompany it, I shall go back to the Pass in the morning.*
>
> *After the levee had been cut, the pilots thought it unsafe to undertake an entrance for several days. The gunboat Forest Rose, needing repairs, ran up to Memphis, returned, and, on the morning of the 7th, we ran down and entered the Pass with great ease. About a mile inside of the levee we struck Moon lake, ran down it about 5 miles, to the point where the Pass leaves it, and from that point I proceeded to make further examinations. I was somewhat disappointed to find the stream neither as large nor straight as it is nearer the river. I went in it about 3 miles in an open boat, but found no obstruction of a serious nature. However, we found three men who had just come through in a dug-out from the Tallahatchie, ostensibly for supplies of salt, &c. They said that the people at the mouth of Coldwater had discovered what had been done at the levee, and that a force of rebels (some 30 or 40), with about 100 negroes, had been engaged for several days in felling timber across the stream at intervals between its junction with the Coldwater and a point nearly 5 miles from Moon Lake.*
>
> *The next day (yesterday), after waiting till noon for a small steamer that I had expected the day before, I went in again with Captain* [G.W.] *Brown's cutter and crew, and descended the Pass nearly 6 miles. During this trip we took 2 men who had belonged to a company of partisan cavalry. They spoke of the rebels having been there in small force, engaged in cutting timber, but said they had left the evening before.*
>
> *I saw, perhaps, at different points, forty trees that had been cut so as to fall in the stream, but in no place had it obstructed the channel so as to resist or prevent the passage of boats. At three places some drift timber had collected against standing trees, so as to contract the water-way, but a few hours' work would open it so as to make the passage easy. The timber, or, at least, all that I saw, which had been cut into so as to hurt nothing. From this fact, and the opinion of boatmen accustomed to small streams, I am inclined to think that, although many more trees may have been cut lower down, and at points opposite each other, they will not materially interfere with navigation.*

The stream is only about 100 feet wide (but very deep), and, as the timber overhangs in many places, it will be necessary to cut out considerable in order to prevent the smoke-stacks of the steamers from being knocked down. This will be a more tedious operation than usual, from the fact that, in many places, the banks of the stream are under water; but, with all these difficulties, no one here entertains a doubt of our being able to work through.

General Gorman sent General Washburn down yesterday with 1,000 men and sent 500 more this morning. They have begun operations. I shall go down myself early in the morning and push matters as rapidly as possible.

Before I left there the ferry-boat Luella, about 100 feet long, had gone into the Pass nearly 3 miles, turned about, and returned....

Should the river fall again 8 or 10 feet, there is not the possibility of a doubt that Yazoo Pass can be opened to admit a large class of boats, and after the Coldwater is reached there are no obstacles of any kind, and very little chance of interposing any, until you arrive at Yazoo City; there is a bluff there, and the next high land is at Haynes' Bluff.[61]

Toward the beginning of the movement into the pass, Captain George W. Brown, acting master of the *Forest Rose*, and Lieutenant Colonel James H. Wilson, Grant's chief topographical engineer, were known to take a skiff ahead of the fleet to reconnoiter. Brown reported on February 7:

This morning at 11:30 AM we entered the pass. We experienced but little difficulty in passing through into Moon Lake, a distance of about one mile; and from there into the mouth of the Old Pass, a distance of about 4 miles, there is a good, wide channel with 4 fathoms and upward. I went on shore and brought three men onboard who had just landed from a skiff. They had come up the pass from the Coldwater. They say that the rebels are felling trees across the pass below. We cannot enter the pass with this boat until the trees are trimmed and some of the overhanging trees cut down. I took my cutter and with an armed crew, went down the pass about one mile, but the strength of the current would not permit our going any farther. We met no serious obstruction, and the prisoners say that it is 4 miles to where the rebels have been at work. There was a party of 10 or 12 cavalry here yesterday. Finding that we could do nothing without a small steamer, we returned and met General Gorman, with the Carl, a small side-wheel steamer, who came in and entered the pass a little way, but it was so late he had to return. He has gone to Helena for a 100 men and axes, etc., and will return early in the morning, when we shall renew our attempt.[62]

The cavalry that Brown and Wilson encountered was Captain Aaron H. Forrest's Cavalry Company of the 6th Battalion, Mississippi State Troops, sent to scout and, if possible, delay the fleet's advance. Aaron Forrest was seven years younger than his famous brother, General Nathan Bedford Forrest. With the rank of captain, Forrest commanded a cavalry company. Operating mostly as scouts, Forrest's company was in the Mississippi Delta in the spring of 1863. Once the Union flotilla entered the Yazoo Pass, men under Forrest's command took shots at the soldiers on board the Union vessels, cut down trees ahead of the fleet and watched and reported on the progress of the Federal expedition.

When Brown and Wilson entered the pass on the *Forest Rose*, Captain Forrest's company was watching from the riverbank, ready to fire on Brown and Wilson. Seeing Wilson's uniform, however, and perhaps confused that Brown's pilot's insignia indicated a Union general, Forrest decided to let the small vessel pass by in the hopes of capturing the whole party; as they were about to spring the trap, however, Forrest's men heard the unmistakable sound of movement in the woods toward the Confederate position. Thinking that he had been outflanked by a Union landing party, Forrest's men fell back. In the meantime, Wilson and Brown escaped the trap laid for them, rejoining the fleet in Moon Lake. Unaware of the danger facing them, Brown and Wilson would have no doubt been captured by the young Captain Forrest if not for a noisy group of wild pigs running through the woods.[63]

Porter had placed Lieutenant Commander Watson Smith in command of the expedition. Porter had great trust in Smith's abilities after he proved himself under fire when he commanded the lead vessel of the lead division in Porter's mortar flotilla during the assault on New Orleans in April 1862. Afterward, Porter appointed Smith commander of the first division of light-draft vessels on January 4, 1863, where Smith served with distinction on the assault of Arkansas Post.[64]

Porter provided Smith with detailed guidance in a February 6 message:

> *Do not enter the Yazoo cut until the current is quite slack; and some small transport will have to go ahead, and the soldiers will have to cut away the trees and branches, so as to not endanger the smokestacks of the steamers.*
>
> *Proceed carefully and only in the daytime; 600 to 800 troops will be detached to accompany you, and you will take 100 aboard each light-draft. See that the army sends a very small steamer, with stores from Helena.*

When you get to the Tallahatchie proceed with all dispatch to ascend it as far as the railroad crossing, and completely destroy the railroad bridge at that point, after which you will, if possible, cut the telegraph wires and proceed down to the mouth of the Yalobusha…dash on to Grenada, destroy completely the railroad bridge, and retire at once down the river without any further damage, excepting to destroy means of transportation (which you will do in all cases) and you will destroy all small boats.

When you get to the Yalobusha, you will proceed with all force down the Yazoo River and endeavor to get into the Sunflower River, where, it is said, all the large steamers are stowed away. These you will not have time to capture; therefore you will destroy them, keeping an account, as near as you can, of the value of the property that falls into your hands.

Obtain all the information that you can in relation to ironclads, and destroy them if you can while they are on the stocks.

If this duty is performed as I expect it to be, we will strike a terrible blow to the enemy, who do not anticipate an attack from such a quarter. But you must guard against surprise and if overwhelmed run your vessels on the bank and set them afire.…By going along only in the daytime, under low steam, you can cruise some time. But after doing the damage, I mentioned in my orders. Ascend the river again to the Yazoo Cut-off, and report to me by a dispatch boat.

You will likely find Honey Island fortified. If it has guns on it, and you can take them, destroy them effectively and destroy the fort.

Do not engage batteries with the light vessels. The Chillicothe will do the fighting. Let me hear from you as soon as possible.[65]

On February 8, Brown reported to Porter:

This morning I got underway and ran up to nearly the head of the lake but discovered nothing. At 1:00 p.m. I manned my cutter and started down the pass. We went 6 or 7 miles…with no serious difficulty in the way. There are some trees that will have to be cut before this boat can enter. The rebels has saved us the trouble by cutting a number themselves.…We met two men, whom we found, upon questioning, belonged to Porter's Company of Mississippi Cavalry. I paroled and allowed them to remain at home.…We returned to our boat and are now on our way to Helena.[66]

On February 13, Smith reported to Porter that Confederate forces were aware of the fleet's presence and its attempt to navigate the Yazoo

Pass. Smith received other reports of Confederate vessels, commanded by Lieutenant Isaac Brown, in the Coldwater River but treated them as rumors. Smith noted in his report, "They were fully apprised of the expedition, before, or as soon as, the work commenced. I was told yesterday by an officer that he heard of it in Memphis. They are in force at Grenada, Panola, and along the lie of railroad, and are already disputing our advance through the Yazoo Pass."[67]

In a message to Brigadier General Benjamin M. Prentiss, commanding at Helena, Arkansas, dated February 15, Grant stated:

> *I send with this, steamers to take on board Gen. Ross' Division to be used in the Yazoo Pass expedition….If this expedition should succeed in getting into the Coldwater I want Gen. Ross to take with him all the force he starts from Helena with…the only change I would make in the instructions already given is that as soon as they arrive at the mouth of the Yalobusha they turn up that steam and take Grenada and destroy the railroad bridges there before proceeding further down river. Let there be no delay in this matter. Time is now growing important.*[68]

On February 24, the waters had calmed and leveled off, allowing Union gunboats and transports to begin moving into the pass. The naval forces of the operation were commanded by Lieutenant Commander Smith. The flotilla consisted of two ironclads, the *Chillicothe* and the *Baron De Kalb*, six tinclads, a ram and fourteen light-draft transports carrying Brigadier General Leonard F. Ross's 13th Division from McClernand's corps. Although Ross had only commanded this division for two weeks prior to this expedition, he was an experienced commander. He served as a lieutenant in the 4th Illinois Volunteers during the Mexican-American War. He had served as a probate judge, county clerk, local politician and stockbreeder before securing a colonelcy in the 17th Illinois on May 25, 1861. Ross commanded his regiment in several minor engagements in the early part of the war, but he came of age as the 3rd Brigade commander in McClernand's Corps at Fort Donelson, which earned him the rank of brigadier general. Although absent for the Battle of Shiloh, he participated in operations around Corinth, Mississippi; Bolivar, Tennessee; and the Mississippi Central Railroad campaign.[69]

The objective of the expedition was to reach Haynes' Bluff before the Confederates were aware of the objective, but Smith was proceeding too cautiously—so much so that it took four days just to navigate fourteen miles between the Mississippi River and the Coldwater and another six days to steam down the Coldwater to the Tallahatchie. Although navigating was difficult at times—with the overhanging trees causing problems for the smokestacks, Confederate snipers shooting at the fleet and the fallen trees cut down to slow the fleet's progress—Smith's lack of urgency for the mission was unjustifiable.

Weeks before the operation got underway, Commander Isaac Brown, former commander of the CSS *Arkansas*, had warned Pemberton that the Yazoo Pass route could be a back door to Vicksburg. Upon hearing that the Federals had cut the Mississippi River levee, Brown took every available man and hurried upriver from the naval yard at Yazoo City. His men felled trees in an attempt to block the channel, but despite his efforts, the Federal fleet crept forward. Between the navy and army engineers, these obstructions were removed. Colonel James H. Wilson sent an entire regiment ashore with cables to haul them away by sheer strength and numbers. It worked so well, he said, that he never afterward wondered how the Egyptians had hauled their great stone blocks to build the pyramids.[70]

As the fleet crept along, many noticed that the levees along the streams provided high grounds for plantation homes to be built on, allowing Union sailors and soldiers to encounter the local citizenry in the area. "Truly we are in an enemy country," said surgeon Henry C. Huntsman of the Fifth Iowa. "Most of the homes seem deserted and where citizens had been sitting about their doors, a sullen silence prevails, no expression or evidence of welcome to our troops."[71]

As the fleet proceeded, Captain Elihu Enos of Company G, 28th Wisconsin Infantry, reported while on board the steamer *St. Louis*, "During the day we passed many splendid plantations, most of them deserted by the white people, and left in the sole possession of the 'colored' population, who greeted us with every demonstration they could think of....In some instances there were the whole black populations of a plantation standing upon the bank, with their bundles, a mule or two, a bale of cotton which they had succeeded in saving from the rebels."[72]

The expeditionary reporter for the *New York Herald* wrote:

> *In the parts of the Coldwater and Tallahatchie mentioned as good, we found high banks and well cultivated plantations in abundance. The owners of these plantations, with their colonies of negroes, were, as a general thing, at home, attending to their ordinary avocations as though there existed no war in the land. At these places we were repeatedly told that the rebels had recently visited them in boats, picking up cotton to be used*

in building fortifications lower down the river to oppose our progress. But we met with no manner of resistance or trouble from any of these people. Their disposition seemed perfectly friendly, and we passed them without further molestation than levying a few hundred bales of cotton from them to strengthen the defences of our gunboats and transports. Of this staple there was no lack in that region, nor had there apparently been any efforts made to conceal or destroy it. This was the more remarkable since the planters admitted that they had been expecting this expedition for a month past. They evidently knew but little of war, and feared it as little. No cotton burners had ever prowled about their gins; no guerillas infested their neighborhood. An invading army had never trod their soil, and even a rebel force had never visited them. It was a single miniature sketch of Southern life as it was before the war.[73]

Throughout the expedition, the soldiers were used to remove obstacles from the pass. Many of the trees removed were cottonwoods, sycamores and cypress that measured about four feet in diameter, weighing thirty-five tons. The best solution was to saw the trees in two and then use some two hundred to four hundred men to pull a six-inch cable to haul trees out. The task was made difficult by exposure and exhaustion, and troops had to continuously be replaced by fresh men from Helena.[74]

During the months of January and February, Pemberton had been

Major General William W. Loring, commanding the Confederate forces at Fort Pemberton. Loring lost his arm during the Mexican-American War (1846–48) leading a charge. He was famous for his line, "Give them Blizzards!" referring the artillery fire on the Union navy attacking Fort Pemberton. *Courtesy the National Archives.*

mirroring Grant's moves by moving the bulk of his troops off the Yalobusha Line at Grenada to Vicksburg. He would leave Major General W.W. Loring's Division at Grenada to keep Major General Stephen E. Hurlbut's corps in check in western Tennessee. Upon learning from Commander Brown that a fleet was moving down the Yazoo Pass, Pemberton ordered Loring to move his men along the south bank of the Yalobusha River to Greenwood and stop the enemy's advance.

Loring was a one-armed veteran of the Mexican-American War and became one of the more troublesome of Confederate generals, frequently engaging in disputes with his superiors. He was nicknamed "Old Blizzards" by his men because of his battle cry, "Give them Blizzards, boys! Give them Blizzards!"

While serving under Robert E. Lee in the first summer of the war, Loring took part in the disappointments of the campaign in western Virginia. That winter, his troops were placed under the overall command of Stonewall Jackson. Following the Romney Campaign, Loring opposed the stationing of his men in the exposed town during the bitter winter and obtained orders from Secretary of War Judah P. Benjamin to move to Winchester. Outraged, Jackson threatened to resign and was eventually upheld in his views of military etiquette. On February 9, 1862, Loring was removed from his post but a few days later was appeased with promotion to major general. Because he continued with his disputes with his superiors, on November 27, 1862, he was transferred to the command of Lieutenant General John C. Pemberton at Jackson, Mississippi.[75]

On February 11, Loring notified Pemberton that he had ordered Major Green L. Blythe to "annoy" the enemy and had ordered General James Z. George's Mississippi State Troops Cavalry forward. Loring asked Pemberton whether forces could be sent from Yazoo City to attack the Federals in the pass. Loring also forwarded a report from Captain J.A. Porter, of the Confederate Engineer Corps, who indicated that a Union ram and several transports were in Moon Lake on February 8. Captain Porter requested artillery and cavalry, stating that "opportunities for attack are good" and that the Coldwater River could not be obstructed "without a steamboat and some chains." After much discussion, Pemberton and Loring both agreed that a detachment should be sent out to search for a suitable spot to build a fort to stop the expedition.[76]

Chapter 4

Location! Location! Location!

The first indication of an enemy that we have met with. They might spare themselves the pains of luring us forward, as we are bound to advance any way. And probably when they get us in that tight place where they expect to entrap us—which is most likely the Yazoo river, between Greenwood and Yazoo City—they will find themselves in possession of an animal of larger proportions than they have calculated on, and I shall be grandly mistaken if they do not find us more than a match. At all events, we are keeping a sharp lookout for them, and shall give them as good a fight as we can whenever we catch them.

—expedition's correspondent, New York Herald[77]

On February 9, Commander Brown forwarded to Pemberton a report notifying Lieutenant General Pemberton that the enemy had cut the Yazoo Pass levee. Brown urged that two big guns be shipped from Mobile to Grenada to establish a defense at the mouth of the Yalobusha River, where enemy gunboats entering from the Tallahatchie River could only attack two abreast. Pemberton replied that the guns would not be sent from Mobile and expressed disbelief that gunboats could get through the pass. He did, however, request a field battery to reinforce the command.[78]

Brown would later forward to Pemberton dispatches from Lieutenant F.E. Sheppard, CSN, that explained how serious the situation was as the Union fleet began to make progress down the pass. Sheppard and his naval party had been working ever since the levee was breeched to obstruct the Yazoo

Pass. On February 14, he wrote, "The enemy has driven us off the works on the Pass, and are coming through. Hasty obstructions with fortifications may save Yazoo City. I have done my best; worked under their noses, till their pickets came within 100 yards of me." Brown also stated that he was outfitting two vessels, the *Mary Keene* and *Star of the West*, but needed men to crew both ships. Brown also expressed concern that he had little time to prepare and that he could "give no assurance that we shall be able to stop the enemy, as we cannot tell with what amount or description of force he is coming through. We will do all we can." Pemberton sent what he could, directed Major General C.L. Stevenson to send two hundred soldiers from Vicksburg to help Commander Brown to man his vessels and sent a thirty-two-pounder rifle and a thirty-pounder to Yazoo City to be placed under Loring's command.[79]

President Jefferson Davis also expressed concern to his Department of the West commander, General Joseph E. Johnston, regarding the opening of the Yazoo Pass. On February 19, while reviewing the troops at Vicksburg with Johnston, Davis expressed the opinion that "the rise of the river…has also opened the line of the Yazoo Pass, and if it has not been sufficiently obstructed, may enable the enemy to come down the Tallahatchie, and get in rear of our position."[80]

Pemberton responded by ordering scouting parties to reconnoiter the area to find a suitable place to build such fortifications. One of those parties was led by Sargent W.A. Gillespie of Company C, 20th Mississippi Infantry. A native of Greenwood and knowledgeable of the area, he was ordered to take a party of civil engineers, overseers and two hundred "negroes" down the Yalobusha and up the Tallahatchie Rivers for the purpose of helping the engineers to locate and fortify a position to stop Commander Smith's fleet.

Gillespie was a resident of Greenwood and knew the surrounding area. The following are his accounts of that expedition as they traveled on the steamboat *Dew Drop* piloted by Sid Auter:

> *We proceeded to the mouth of the Yazoo Pass, where the overseers and negroes were landed on both sides of the pass to obstruct the same and thereby prevent the fleet from descending, when Captain W.B. Prince, in command of a cavalry company above us…sent us word to leave at once or we would be captured, and that by cutting down the overhanging trees we were helping the enemy more than ourselves, as the fleet had a submarine saw boat in advance, which sawed the trees up and floated them to one side out of their way. So we took on board the overseers and the Negroes and*

left there in a hurry and steamed down to the mouth of Coldwater River, where the engineers landed and examined the ground for fortifications and pronounced it unsuitable. We then proceeded down the Tallahatchie River out of what is known as the "Wilderness," to about Sharkey Landing and tied up for the night. Late in the night while everyone was asleep except the watchman, pilot, mate, and myself, who were playing cards my partner began to complain that I was not taking interest in the game and making bad plays. I replied, "I was thinking more about helping the engineers out of their trouble in selecting a suitable place to fortify." I remarked to Auter, who was somewhat acquainted with the topography of the country, that the mouth of Clayton Bayou would be the most suitable in my judgement. So we awoke the engineers and stated the case to them who, becoming very much interested, kept me up the balance of the night in mapping of the ground and propounding questions to me. Just before daylight they ordered Capt. Sturdivant to get up steam and proceed to the mouth of Clayton Bayou at once, when the Captain and pilot protested that it was very dark and there were no torch lights aboard, to which the engineers replied, "D---it, float till daylight," which we did, and on arriving at Clayton Bayou that evening the engineers landed and after looking over the ground and verifying the maps of the country with aid of some citizens, they commenced to stake off the ground in a zig-zag way for the breastworks and named the place Ft. Pemberton.[81]

After dispatches were sent to Loring to bring his division to Greenwood, orders were given to *Dew Drop* and other boats to travel up and down the Tallahatchie to Curtis Plantation and the Purnell Plantation, after a load of cotton bales to be used as breastworks. Private Ernst Knolle of Company C, 1st Battalion, Waul's Texas Legion, recorded that "on this place breastworks were made by putting from 3 to 5 cotton-bales on top of one another, and some 4 or 5 bales wide. After this, then dirt was thrown on the bales, which made very good breastworks."[82] The fort was a line of earthworks that extended across the narrow strip of land between the Tallahatchie and Yazoo Rivers. The works were approximately 2,500 feet in length, erected at approximately a forty-five-degree angle from northeast to southwest. The angle in the bend of the Tallahatchie would allow the Confederate gunners a commanding control of the river for about one thousand yards. The immediate area of the fort was about 2 feet above the level of the rivers. The battery platforms were 4 feet high and were protected by parapets that were 10 feet high.[83]

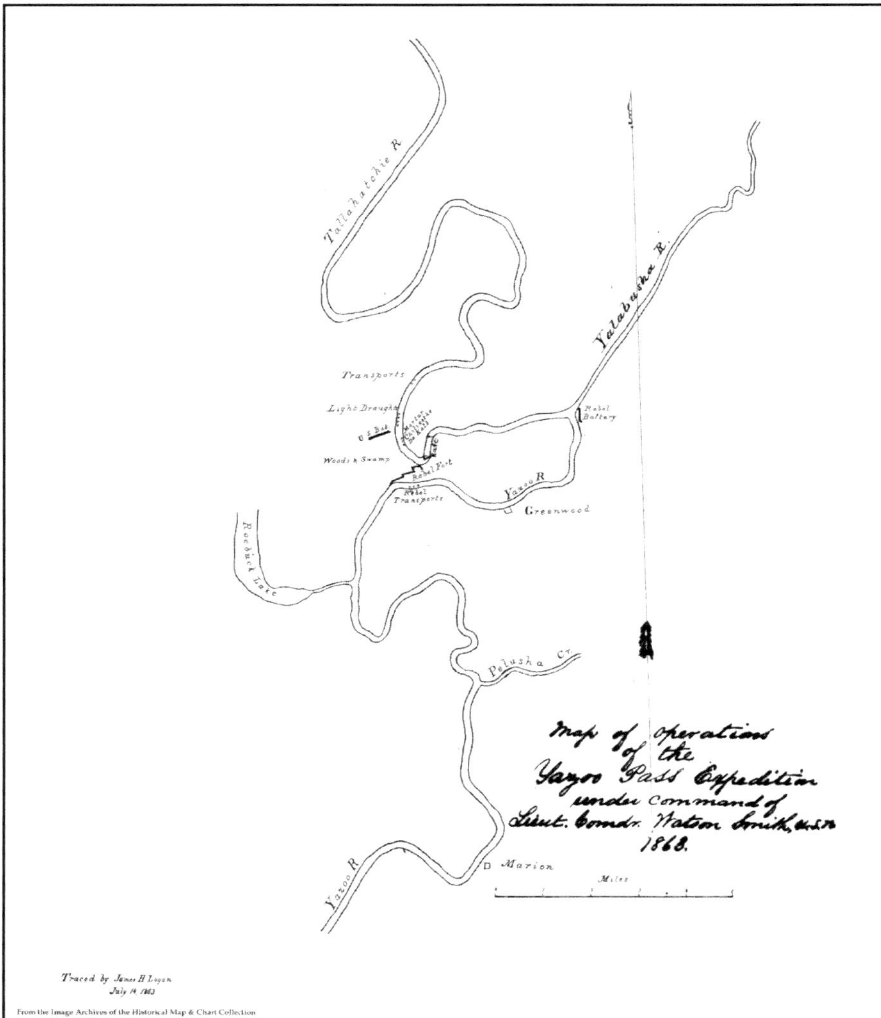

Confederate general W.W. Loring's battle map showing the Union and Confederate lines that accompanied his reports. *Courtesy of www.aboutgreenwoodms.com/fort-pemberton.html.*

Loring arrived at Greenwood on February 21 to examine the fortifications being constructed by the engineers. He reported to Pemberton that the defenses would be established in the vicinity of Beck's Ferry, about four miles by water below Greenwood, and that it would be an excellent choice. The fort sits on a peninsula that forms a *U* shape in the bend of the river. The

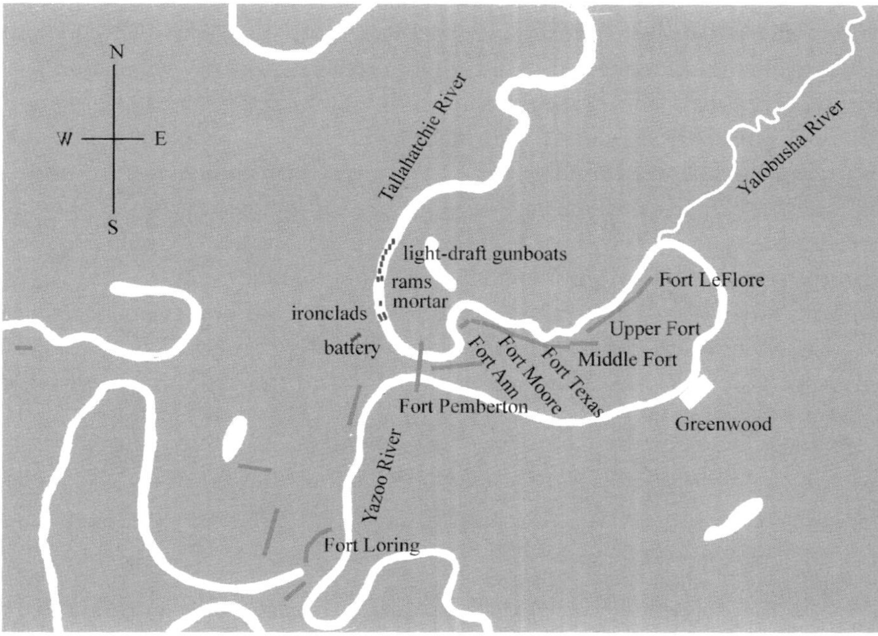

A map of the location of Fort Pemberton and other defenses if the Union army were to get past the fort. *Courtesy of city-data.com.*

fields surrounding the fort had been cleared in case of attack by infantry, which in addition to having to cross the open fields would also have to ford Clayton's Bayou. Works commanding each river were to be connected by lines of rifle pits and entrenchments. Loring reported that the riverbanks were eight feet above the water, and the guns were being mounted on earth and cotton bale works. He believed that this would provide enough elevation to ensure plunging fire on the Federal boats. The Tallahatchie and Yazoo Rivers at this point were only five hundred yards apart.[84]

During this time, Loring began receiving troops into his command. Colonel Thomas N. Waul's Texas Legion had moved into Greenwood from Snyder's Bluff the previous week. Waul's defensive arrangements were approved by Loring, and Waul was placed in command of the defense force. Other units began pouring into Greenwood, creating an initial force of about two thousand men under Loring's command.[85]

By March 11, Fort Pemberton contained seven guns mounted *en barbette*, behind breastworks. The heavy weapons included one banded thirty-two-pounder rifle, one twelve-pounder rifle, one three-inch Whitworth gun, two twelve-pounder rifles on siege carriages, one three-inch Parrot gun and one twenty-pounder Parrot gun. Lighter cannons included one six-pounder at the center of the fort and one six-pounder and one three-inch rifle placed on the left flank of the fort. There were three cotton bale/earth magazines spread out in the fort, which were constructed to supply the guns with ammunition.[86]

Gillespie had chosen the site well. Fort Pemberton was well defended against an approach down the Tallahatchie from the north. No more than two vessels could approach the fort at one time. If the fort was approached by land, an infantry assault would have to cross six hundred yards of cleared ground and bayou. Any woods bordering the cleared fields were in effective

Opposite, top: "Lady Polk" authentication. *Courtesy of Annette McCluney.*

Opposite, bottom: "Lady Polk." *Courtesy of Annette McCluney.*

Below: "Lady Polk," a three-inch rifle cannon, was placed on its original gun platform in Fort Pemberton. This Blakely cannon is the only working cannon of its kind today and was an original gun at Fort Pemberton. *Courtesy of Annette McCluney.*

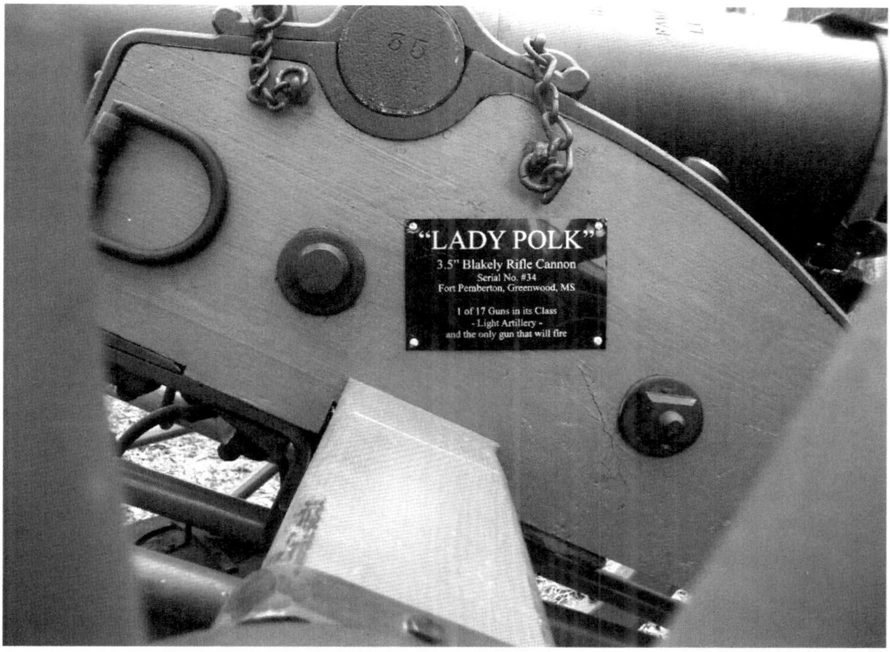
"LADY POLK"
3.5" Blakely Rifle Cannon
Serial No. #34
Fort Pemberton, Greenwood, MS
1 of 17 Guns in its Class
- Light Artillery -
and the only gun that will fire

"Lady Polk," looking down the barrel toward the bend of the river where the Federal gunboats appeared. *Courtesy of Annette McCluney.*

range of all batteries. Loring also ordered a raft to be constructed across the river abreast of the fort and the *Star of the West* scuttled directly behind it in the channel to block passage of the gunboats.

Loring ordered steamboats moving supplies to Grenada and Vicksburg on the Yalobusha and Yazoo Rivers to be allowed to continue their operations unhindered. Any steamboats that were not being required to transport supplies were to be converted to serve as "cottonclad" troop transports under the command of Captain Brown. The cottonclads would also be used to attack and board any Federal boats that might get past Greenwood.[87]

While construction of Fort Pemberton was being completed, groups of cavalry scouts were buying Loring the necessary time to complete the works and assemble his force. On February 23, Captain Thomas Henderson reported, "Today the Federals were working on the last blockade in the Yazoo Pass, and finished clearing it out by the afternoon. About 4 o'clock they entered the Coldwater. One gunboat and three transports are at the mouth of the pass. They have a force of about 3,000 infantry and 300 cavalry camped within three miles above the mouth of the pass. The obstructions placed in the Coldwater below the pass have been washed off by the high water."

On March 2, Admiral Porter sent a report to U.S. Secretary of the Navy Gideon Wells stating, "Our expedition across to the Tallahatchie, through Yazoo Pass, is succeeding and we have 10 vessels, at last accounts, within a short distance of the Tallahatchie. Officers and men, assisted by the troops, working with a determination that nothing can conquer, and driving the enemy before them. There are but few troops in Vicksburg at this moment, and matters look prosperous."[88]

Loring reported that same day that the Federal force on the Yazoo Pass had grown substantially from the report he received on February 26: "The bearer of a flag of truce to enemy at Yazoo Pass on the 26th reports: Saw six stern-wheel and one side-wheel gunboats near where pass empties into Coldwater. No gunboat had yet been in the Coldwater, and tug passed into Coldwater and returned; intention to bring gunboats through evident. There were about 7,000 troops on a large number of transports on Moon Lake. Enemy gunboats have 24-pounder in bow, with iron plating to protect."[89]

On March 5, after receiving positive reports, Grant decided to reinforce the expedition by sending Major General James B. McPherson's XVII Corp, then located at Lake Providence, Louisiana. It was Grant's intention to create a lodgment on the east bank of the Yazoo River so that a coordinated attack could be carried out on Vicksburg with his entire army. Grant told McPherson:

> *I want your corps to get there as quickly as possible, and effect a lodgment at Yazoo City, or the most eligible point on the Yazoo River from which to operate.... Quinby will have general direction in the Pass until you arrive. He may detain Ross' Division, now there, until there are sufficient forces to defend his position.... I will give orders to Denver's Division to...go in the same route. This will give you five Divisions to operate with, which, with the Gunboats. I hope will enable you to carry out one end of the proposed programs.*[90]

The 7th Division had 311 officers and 5,539 men present for duty. They had almost finished a completed planned maneuver down Mississippi River from Memphis, Tennessee, to Grand Lake. Quinby and his staff had the troops re-embark at Grand Lake on March 7 and traveled some two hundred miles back upriver, arriving at Moon Lake by March 9. However, upon arrival, there were insufficient troop transports at the pass. Quinby would have wait for additional transports from Helena, Arkansas.

Grant also requested additional small transports on March 5 to move Quinby's men. The quartermaster sent all available boats, as well as shallow-draft steamboats, as fast as possible from the Ohio and Mississippi Rivers. This forced Quinby to delay his advance again until March 14, when his 1st Brigade, led by Colonel John Sanborn, entered the Yazoo Pass. Quinby wrote to McPherson that flatboats would have been better suited for the task than small steamboats.[91]

Once the additional transports arrived, their generally poor construction was noted. One eyewitness reported:

> *There has been much said of the frauds practiced upon the government by contractors and agents at the East in purchasing and chartering transports for the several coastwise expeditions that have been fitted out....I would suggest that these investigations be extended to the chartering of vessels on the Western rivers. I am confident that such an investigation would be productive of the most profitable results. Take, for example, the vessels chartered for this expedition....They are nearly all old, broken down, water logged boats that can scarcely be kept afloat in any water. For an expedition of this nature stout, serviceable boats were required that would stand a good deal of thumping and knocking about in these narrow, crooked streams. We have been delayed most provokingly by reason of these boats breaking down. One or two of them have been finally condemned and sent back to Helena. Others have to lay by constantly to repair and patch up, so as to be able to get along. Of course when this occurs there is a gap made in the fleet, or else the whole expedition must wait for them. Somebody is to blame for sending such boats, and doubtless somebody pockets a good price for securing charters for these old tubs. I don't pretend to know who the culpable party is; but I do know that had we been provided with better and stronger boats we could now have been twice as far on our way. The steamer Raymond left Helena a week ago with commissary stores. She sprang a leak in the Yazoo Pass, and was obliged to throw half her stores overboard to save the rest. The little ferry boat Carl overtook her three days ago and brought forward the greater part of the freight the Raymond had left. The Raymond has not yet caught up with us. So it seems that somebody is still chartering unseaworthy boats. The matter ought to be looked into.*[92]

As the expedition continued to slowly advance down the Coldwater and Tallahatchie Rivers, Smith noted that the fleet was moving at about one and a half miles per hour. Almost every ship had suffered some type of damage from overhanging trees on their smokestacks, since they measured almost twenty feet tall. The gunboats seemed to fair somewhat better, but the captain of *Chillicothe* did note that a snag had loosened a plank in its hull.[93]

Both Ross and Wilson were disgusted at the slow, cautious progress that the fleet was making. Ross was so annoyed that he expressed his concerns to Prentiss: "We have again made a late start this morning, being delayed for the gunboats to complete coaling. The work should have been done by 2 o'clock this morning, and we on our way by 5:30, but it was 7:30 this morning before we started, and then had to leave one of the gunboats to finish her coaling. I am a little, yes, considerably disgusted with these necessary delays."[94]

Ross used much stronger language about the delays in his after-action report dated April 18:

> *On several occasions the gunboat immediately in my advance stopped and lay to an hour for dinner. In consulting with Lieutenant Commander Watson Smith, I urged the necessity of greater rapidity of movement, advised leaving the coal-barges in the rear…and, with the ironclads and such light transports and light gunboats as could keep up with them, to push forward with the utmost expedition, and gain the mouth of the Tallahatchie, and hold it until the rest of the fleet could catch up with them.*[95]

Wilson expressed concerns about the progress of Smith in his after-action report to Rawlins dated March 15: "When the ironclads started into the pass, I urged with all the force that I could the absolute necessity of sending them, the rams and the two mosquitoes forward with all possible dispatch. Foster, Walker, and General Ross agreed with the plan. Had this been done, they could have reached the mouth of the Tallahatchie in four days."[96]

A newspaper reporter for the *New York Herald* who was traveling with the expedition noted:

> *After passing down the Tallahatchie about twenty-five miles, its banks become low, and at the present high stage of the water are sadly overflown. We then travelled for forty or fifty miles with scarcely a break in the wilderness. Not a plantation is to be seen on either hand. The course of the stream became exceedingly tortuous, the bends sharp and abrupt, the timber scraggy and hanging far over the water, and the whole appearance wild*

> *and forbidding. We have just emerged from this desolation, and are now steaming along, at a fair rate of speed, in a moderately wide and straight river, with frequent plantations of considerable pretensions along the banks. Here we begin to discover the handiwork of the enemy. At nearly every one of these plantations we find a huge, smoking, smoldering pile of what was but recently cotton worth a dollar a pound. These gins and cotton piles have evidently been but recently fired, evidencing that the enemy are close in front of us, most probably falling back before us to lure us on to what they may consider our sure destruction. It is the first indication of an enemy that we have met with. They might spare themselves the pains of luring us forward, as we are bound to advance any way. And probably when they get us in that tight place where they expect to entrap us, which is most likely the Yazoo river, between Greenwood and Yazoo City, they will find themselves in possession of an animal of larger proportions than they have calculated on, and I shall be grandly mistaken if they do not find us more than a match. At all events, we are keeping a sharp lookout for them, and shall give them as good a fight as we can whenever we catch them.*[97]

On March 9, the expedition surprised Commander Brown's Confederate transports *St. Mary's* and the *Thirty-Fifth Parallel* about seventy miles above the junction of the Tallahatchie and Yalobusha Rivers while collecting cotton bales for a cottonclad fleet he was building; Brown was forced to make a hasty retreat downriver. During the retreat, he lost the *Thirty-Fifth Parallel* when it ran aground, and Brown was forced to set the vessel and its cargo of between 2,500 and 3,000 bales of cotton on fire. The reporter for the *New York Herald* reported the incident:

> *Yesterday afternoon the side-wheel steamer Parallel was cruising along fifteen or twenty miles above here, and had picked up an immense load of cotton, supposed to be not less than three thousand bales. While engaged in gathering her load of cotton the smoke of our approaching fleet was discovered curling up in heavy black masses over the heavy timber. She immediately turned about and made all possible speed downstream; but in turning a sharp bend in the river she manifested more haste than wisdom, and ran afoul of a large tree, which so disabled her that she was unable to proceed any further. Her officers and crew therefore abandoned her, previously setting her on fire, and when our fleet overhauled her she was completely enveloped in flames, and subsequently proved a total loss. Large quantities of her cotton fell overboard, the water extinguishing the flames, so that for*

> *several miles in that vicinity the river was covered with floating cotton bales. This is now being gathered up by our boat for additional protection to our gunboats. In this capacity it will be of immense service to us.*[98]

As the expedition neared the junctions of the Tallahatchie and Yalobusha Rivers during a hard rainstorm on March 10, Smith was informed about the strength of the Confederates who were awaiting his fleet and ready to defend an area near Greenwood. He was also told that a fort had been constructed and guns had been mounted; a raft had also been constructed as an obstruction. The fort was heavily garrisoned.[99]

The Federal expedition through Yazoo Pass was not going well. Although the last of the ships broke through the strangling pass on March 2, the journey from there, while easier, was anything but speedy. Many of the rations aboard the ships had spoiled, and frequent stops to forage at riverside plantations had to be made to replace them. All along the way, Rebel guerrillas shot from the shores, forcing the Federals to keep their heads down.[100]

All the while, they heard rumors, mostly from slaves, that the Confederates had constructed some sort of fortification in Yazoo City or Greenwood. Lieutenant Commander Smith, overseeing the naval side of the expedition, paid no mind. He simply didn't believe it.[101]

It seems that General Leonard Ross, commanding the infantry on the ships, didn't buy it, either. He assumed that he could be in Greenwood by the tenth. But on that day, they were thirty miles away from Greenwood, and even more rumors—specific rumors—were taking shape. Slaves told of extensive Confederate fortifications at Greenwood. In the water, they said, Rebels had placed obstructions, including rafts and fires, and even the *Star of the West* had been sunk in order to prevent the Federal fleet from passing.[102]

Although General Ross commanded the infantry, he was not the overall commander of the Yazoo Pass Expedition. That task was given to General Isaac Quinby, division commander in James McPherson's XVII Corps. Quinby and his division were preparing to load up and join Ross. When they did, Quinby would take over.

By this point, Ross had probably received Quinby's strong suggestion to be careful. "He [General Grant] evidently attaches great importance to the movement down the Yazoo river," wrote Quinby, "the failure of which would in all probability render it necessary to make a complete change in the present programme, and, to say the least, delay for a long time the accomplishment of our immediate object."[103]

Chapter 5

Give Them Blizzards![104]

By March 11, the Federal fleet was ten miles north of Greenwood at Curtis Plantation. After so many obstacles to overcome, the fleet was in striking distance of Fort Pemberton. An eyewitness reported:

> *We arrived at this point at about nine o'clock this morning. Here we are ten miles above Greenwood, and but two and a half miles from the rebel works. The rebel position is more clearly defined in the map I send you with this. Just below our position the river turns to the eastward, and after describing a wide horseshoe bend again resumes its southerly course at a point nearly south of this. The neck formed by this bend, or rather the base of the peninsula, is something less than a mile across. Directly in this neck the rebels have thrown up their fortifications. These are not so formidable in themselves as might be supposed. They consist of a single line of breastworks composed of cotton bales and earth, facing westerly, and flanked on the right by quite a heavy battery fronting the river and mounting three siege guns. Besides these they seem to have several small field pieces in position. Directly on the right flank of this line of defence they have constructed a raft of logs as a blockade of the river to prevent our boats from running by their batteries.*
>
> *The ground upon which these works are built is as high as any to be found in this region. It is probably elevated above any possible overflow; but with the river as high as it is at present it is but two or three feet above the water level.*

> *Directly in front of their line of breastworks there is quite a deep slough, extending across the neck, and admirably serving the purpose of the ditch usually dug around fortifications. This slough is close to the base of their works at the upper end, but gradually recedes from them until at the lower end it is several hundred feet removed. Still beyond this slough there is an almost impenetrable and very extensive canebrake, with a deep forest reaching far back into the country. About six miles below this fortification, and directly in the arc of the bend, is the confluence of the Yallobusha and Tallahatchie rivers, and from that point down to the Mississippi the joint stream takes the name of the Yazoo river. The little village or settlement of Le Flore lies directly at the junction of the two streams. Greenwood lies upon the Yazoo, four miles below.*[105]

On the morning of March 11, the Federal flotilla of eight gunboats, two rams and a number of troop transports arrived within several miles of Fort Pemberton. General Ross joined Lieutenant Commander Smith and Lieutenant Colonel James Wilson aboard the *Chillicothe* to mull over what to do. The fort they did not believe would be there was there, but it was so far off in the distance they couldn't tell how much of a fort it was. And so they decided to take the *Chillicothe* downstream to reconnoiter the rebel position. The 46th Indiana was sent out on reconnaissance. The men soon encountered Rebel pickets and skirmished in the woods briefly before the Confederates began retreating to the safety of their fort. The 28th Wisconsin was ordered down the west bank of the river in support of the 46th Indiana. Sergeant Lauren Barker of Company A, 48th Wisconsin, had this to say as his regiment went into battle:

> *We landed yesterday two miles above here, and marched down here about 3 P.M. The gunboats were one or two of them in advance. While we were marching down, one of the gunboats opened on the Rebel battery, which almost immediately replied, and here we had our first sight & heard the first sounds of real war.…The first shot fell just at my left and opposite the head of my company, as we were marching down the river bank, striking the water about 4 rods from me. The next passed just over our heads. The third struck a tree in front, bringing down some dead limbs about Col. Lewis' horse's heels.*[106]

At the same time, the ironclad *Chillicothe* steamed into view of the fort and began lobbing eleven-inch shells. As the ship moved closer, they could see that the Confederate position was an earthen fort, sitting low to the ground. It had been constructed of dirt and bales of cotton and was so designed that it spanned the entire point on the bend of the river, anchoring its right (northern flank) to the Tallahatchie River, while its left (southern flank) held tight to the Yazoo, which was formed when the Tallahatchie and Yalobusha Rivers met.

Eight Rebel cannons dotted the embrasures, nearly one thousand yards in length. Their largest gun was a thirty-two-pounder, which, though on the left (southern flank), had a clear shot all the way up the Tallahatchie as far as the eye could see. The other guns had a smaller field of fire, but not by much.[107]

As the Federals approached, Colonel Robert McCulloch's 2nd Missouri Cavalry was ordered to fall back to the south bank of the Yalobusha River.[108] Smith continued to move downstream on board the *Chillicothe*, accompanied by Ross and Wilson. Just as his ship rounded the bend at about eight hundred to nine hundred yards from the Confederate works, the Confederates opened fire with five cannons. The Confederate batteries fired twenty-five to thirty rounds in thirty minutes, but the *Chillicothe* was struck only twice. The first round struck its port bow just above the waterline, but a second struck so heavily that it caused serious damage to the casemate. After firing three rounds from its eleven-inch guns, Smith ordered a withdrawal in an effort to organize a plan of attack. Smith also ordered a damage report of the *Chillicothe* and found the damage more severe than previously thought. Its iron plating and bolts were loosened, and its nine-inch white pine backing was cracked. The Confederates suffered no losses, but the Federals suffered one injury during the reconnaissance of the fort's works and armaments.[109]

General Ross returned to his transports and ordered his 1st Brigade commander, Brigadier General Frederick Salomon, to determine the extent of the Confederate positions. Salomon deployed the 46th and 47th Indiana Infantry. Those two regiments moved forward and approached within three-quarters of a mile of Fort Pemberton. Soldiers from the 46th Indiana met Colonel Waul's Texas Legion pickets and forced the Texans to withdraw. Ross's division disembarked at the Shell Mound plantation, about two miles upstream from Fort Pemberton on the west bank of the Tallahatchie River. The 33rd Iowa Infantry moved upstream on board its transport and fired shots at a squad of Rebels. The remainder of the infantry stayed in the vicinity of the Shell Mound plantation during the day and boarded their vessels that night without being engaged.[110]

That evening, the *Chillicothe* and *Baron De Kalb* began moving downstream again to attack, while the *Lioness* was held in reserve. Once in range, the

Confederate batteries opened fire. After just seven minutes, the *Chillicothe* was forced to withdraw after firing only four rounds. It was preparing to fire a fifth when a Confederate shell entered the open gunport and struck the eleven-inch shell as it was being loaded. Both shells exploded. This explosion killed four men and wounded ten. Two of the *Chillicothe*'s port covers were blown outward by the explosion. A portion of its pine turret backing was carried away, and cotton bales added for protection were set on fire. The eleven-inch gun, although struck on the muzzle, was undamaged. Lieutenant Commander Watson Smith ordered a withdrawal. The Confederates nearly exhausted their rifled thirty-two-pounder ammunition during this engagement but suffered no casualties.[111]

The river was so narrow that the *Chillicothe* and *Baron De Kalb* were forced to fight side by side. Their inability to maneuver caused them to take a terrible pounding. The light-draft gunboats could not engage the batteries since they were forced to remain upstream behind the ironclads. During the night of March 11, about 1,200 soldiers from the 2nd Brigade, commanded by Brigadier General Clinton B. Fisk, dragged three hundred cotton bales and one thirty-pounder Parrott gun from the *Rattler* and created a land battery. During the night of March 12, a second thirty-pounder was added from the *Forest Rose.* This gun position was located about six hundred yards from Fort Pemberton in the woods near the west bank of the Tallahatchie.[112]

March 12, and the morning of March 13, was spent adding cotton to the *Chillicothe* and *Baron DeKalb* to provide additional protection. The *Chillicothe*'s damage was repaired as much as possible under the circumstances. The side port covers were substituted for the forward port covers, and replacement gun crews were transferred to the *Chillicothe* from the *Petrel* and *Signal.*

The Federals renewed their attack on March 13. Two thirty-pound Parrott rifles and a twelve-pound howitzer opened a terrific fire on the Confederate position. Only seven hundred yards away, the Federal gunners could easily find their marks. Twenty minutes later, the USS *Chillicothe* and *Baron De Kalb* steamed toward the fort. Positioned as it was at a narrow pass in the river, only two gunboats could attack it at once. Behind them was a mortar boat that had been towed down from Yazoo Pass and held at the ready. Seeing the Federal ships approaching, Loring ordered his batteries to fire. Less than five minutes later, the *Chillicothe* responded with its starboard gun and, soon after, its port. When it found the mark, it dropped anchor and pounded the Rebel works with its starboard side. With the *Baron De Kalb* beside it, they rang in the noon hour with exploding shells and shrapnel.[113]

At the same time, five companies of the 28th Wisconsin Volunteer Infantry made their approach to the fort. Sergeant Baker reported:

> *Several days were spent skirmishing and getting ready to take the fort. A council of officers was held and it was decided that the two gunboats, Chillicothe and Baron De Kalb, with the land battery we had made, could silence the guns in Fort Pemberton, and then a good storming party could capture the fort. Five companies of the 28th were chosen for this duty, and they went on board the gunboat Signal while the other boats opened fire on the fort.... [W]e marched into the woods toward the fort with our drum corps playing a lively tune and the Rebel shell screaming over our heads. We had not gone far into the woods when the enemy got range on us by the sound of the music and sent a sixty-four pound shot that lodged in a large oak tree just in front of the regiment, and I often think how many lives that tree saved for us.*[114]

After the naval bombardment and a failed infantry assault on Fort Pemberton, part of the 28th Wisconsin boarded a steamboat and was sent ten miles back up the river; there it disembarked and marched ten more miles to McNutt, Mississippi, the county seat of Sunflower County at that time. Its mission was to reconnoiter, forage and disperse a force of Confederate cavalry. The remainder of the regiment was used in a second attack on the fort.[115]

Upon hearing of the approaching Federal soldiers, settlers around the courthouse in McNutt became terrified and immediately set to the task of hiding anything that might look desirable to the enemy. A small fight took place in which the 28th Wisconsin came out ahead and accomplished its mission. Corporal Wildish reported, "We took twelve prisoners and as many horses." Sergeant Sawyer also reported the capturing of Confederate mail as well. Afterward, the 28th Wisconsin marched back to its boat and rejoined the detached companies on the outskirts of Greenwood.[116]

The air inside the earthen Confederate fort was on fire. The garrison troops hugged the ground as the Confederate artillerymen gave as good as they got. An eleven-inch shell from the *Chillicothe* plunged through one of the fort's parapets and ignited one of the Rebel gun's magazines. Fortunately, the shell was faulty and didn't explode, but the burning fuse caught the powder in the cartridges on fire. The flash wounded Lieutenant J.Q. Wall of the Pointe Coupee Artillery and fifteen men of his detachment who were close enough to be burned—some badly.[117]

The Confederate fire mostly ignored the land battery, the mortar boat and the *De Kalb*. Instead, the Rebels focused on the *Chillicothe*, as it was doing most of the damage. Three times Southern shells caught the timber-boned ship on fire. It was hit thirty-eight times, with ten shells landing within the span of ten feet. Seven burst through the wheel housing, which was poorly shielded with twelve-inch-thick wood. But still it stood, firing shot after shot into the Rebel works, though to little effect. Only one shell burst over a Confederate gun, killing one and wounding two others.[118]

With its cotton bales on fire and the wooden portions of the ship being torn away, it soon became obvious that the *Chillicothe* could not reduce Fort Pemberton. Its ammunition running low, the battered and stricken vessel was recalled, leaving the *Baron De Kalb* to stand on its own. General Loring, too, was running low on ammunition. When he saw that the Federal gunboat was pulling back, he slackened and finally stopped. Meanwhile, the *Baron De Kalb* fired once every fifteen minutes, just to remind the Rebels that it was there. "We have lost some valuable gunners and a few others," reported Loring to his commander, General John Pemberton. "Thank God, our losses are so small. Enemy's losses must be great."[119]

But Federal losses were even smaller, with two killed and four wounded aboard the *Chillicothe*. General Ross marveled over the intense fighting. "We have no means of knowing the extent of the enemy's damage," he reported that evening. "If no greater than our own, I may truly say that nobody was hurt by today's operations."

Ross was more or less correct. He was beginning to realize that Fort Pemberton might be a fairly tough nut to crack. Likewise, although the *Chillicothe* had suffered some damage, he didn't think it was so bad. The conclusion was simple: the contest would be a stalemate. But those on board the *Chillicothe*, like its captain, Lieutenant Commander James Foster, held an understandably different opinion. This wouldn't be a stalemate, but a Confederate victory. "The *Chillicothe* is now in condition to engage the enemy," wrote Foster the following day. "She is, however, badly battered and shattered, and does not withstand the enemy's shot and shell near as well as expected." And though the Federals did not know it, after dark, General Loring and his Confederates received a much-needed resupply of ammunition for the big guns. As on the twelfth, the next two days allowed both sides time to refit and repair, with only brief explosions of fighting. Pemberton wrote to Loring that a twenty-pounder Parrott and an eight-inch navy gun were being sent, along with ammunition. Pemberton also wrote that he was trying to get another eight-inch navy gun and a forty-two-pounder. A new attack was coming, and both sides could sense it.[120]

Throughout these operations, Smith's health was failing. He had been ill when he received orders to command the expedition, and his health failed completely during the assaults on Fort Pemberton. On the Union gunboat *Rattler*, Smith was so shaken by the ensuing racket from the shells hitting his ship that he fainted. When he recovered, his men thought him insane, as he began speaking gibberish and giving orders that were unintelligible to his men. One set of orders, issued before his men realized the depth of their commander's mental difficulties, ordered the *Chillicothe* to withdraw from action. On March 17, Smith ordered the flotilla to return upstream and reported himself unfit for duty in a message to Porter. He then departed for Helena on the *Rattler*. On March 19, the *Rattler* was fired on by Confederate forces and lost two men killed. Smith arrived at Helena on March 22 and died shortly thereafter.[121]

Lieutenant Commander James P. Foster of the *Chillicothe* assumed command of the flotilla on March 18. The *Chillicothe* was badly damaged and low on ammunition. The *Baron De Kalb* and mortar raft were low on ammunition, and all vessels were low on provisions. The flooded terrain did not permit land maneuvers, and the gunboats had failed in their duels with Fort Pemberton. Foster ordered the flotilla to return to Helena after consulting with Generals Ross, Fisk and Salomon. The flotilla began to move upstream on March 19.[122]

One officer expressed his disappointment in a diary entry: "A more dissatisfied set of men I never saw…would willingly have stormed the fort rather than left without a more thorough effort to take it.…We could have taken it if our leaders would have but gave us the opportunity."

On March 21, the flotilla encountered Brigadier General Isaac F. Quinby's forces moving downstream to reinforce the expedition. Quinby met with Ross, assumed command of the army forces and ordered Ross to accompany him downriver. His intent was to disembark all army forces near Fort Pemberton and send the transports back to Moon Lake to pick up the remainder of his division. During a separate meeting, he convinced Foster to attempt a supporting attack with the gunboats.[123]

Confederate defenders had been busy during the brief time the expedition had been gone. They had continued to improve Fort Pemberton and had burned the cotton parapet of the Federal shore battery position. Most of the trees near the position had been destroyed during earlier engagements, and the position was now exposed to Confederate fire. About six floating mines were placed in the Tallahatchie.[124]

On March 23, the Federal forces approached Fort Pemberton during a hard rain. *Chillicothe* fired three rounds at Fort Pemberton in an effort to draw fire, but the Confederates did not respond. An underwater mine appeared to detonate as the *Chillicothe* withdrew but caused no damage. Confederate artillery fired at Ross's division, mortally wounding a soldier from the 48th Indiana.[125]

With the stagnation of the Yazoo Pass Expedition, Grant began looking for another way to outflank the Confederates at Vicksburg. Even before the Federal flotilla engaged the Rebels at Fort Pemberton, Admiral Porter had devised another way to use the route through Steele's Bayou to reach the

Right: USS *Carondelet. Courtesy of WCNB.*

Below: USS *Louisville. Courtesy the Library of Congress.*

USS *Black Hawk. Courtesy the Library of Congress.*

Yazoo River, thus bypassing Haynes' Bluff. The whole point of the Yazoo Pass idea was to steam down the Coldwater, Tallahatchie and Yazoo Rivers to come in behind Vicksburg. Since Fort Pemberton blocked the way, that expedition was about to fail. Porter's idea was to bypass the Confederate batteries and steer clear of Fort Pemberton. To do this, he wanted to take five ironclads—*Louisville*, *Carondolet*, *Mound City*, *Pittsburgh* and the *Black Hawk*—up the Yazoo to Steele's Bayou, well before the Rebel batteries. From there, they would steam north to Deer Creek and finally move past Rolling Fork to the Big Sunflower River, which they would take south. It would empty back into the Yazoo River downstream from Yazoo City but well upstream from the batteries. The way would be twisted and far from easy, but he had faith that it could be done.[126]

Grant received word from Vicksburg that the Yazoo Pass Expedition had reached Fort Pemberton and exchanged shots with the Rebel fortifications. He also knew that Fort Pemberton was being reinforced with more troops and guns. Grant felt that if he could move forces between Greenwood and Vicksburg, it would confuse the Confederates at Fort Pemberton and save Ross's force from destruction. At the invitation of Porter, Grant boarded Porter's flagship, the *Black Hawk*, and on March 15 traversed with Porter and ordered Sherman to take his corps "as far as practicable up Steele's Bayou and through Black Bayou to Deer Creek, and…get into the Yazoo River for the purpose of determining the feasibility of getting an army through that route to the east bank of that river, and at a point at which they can act advantageously against Vicksburg." Porter, however, was impatient and left on March 16, before Sherman was ready. There were not enough troop transports to carry his troops, thus creating a gap between army and navy forces as the gunboats proceeded alone.[127]

The trek through Steele's Bayou was rough and got worse the farther they went, but the flotilla finally reached Deer Creek. From there, it could take the narrow waterway south, and it would let them out near the Confederate batteries. The original plan was to take Deer

Creek north to Rolling Fork and Big Sunflower River. Sherman, and his troops, had finally joined Porter by March 21. He preferred to take the route south, the quicker path toward the enemy. Porter, on the other hand, wanted to stick to the original plan. Sherman conceded and returned to his troops, still sloshing through the swamps and bayous toward Deer Creek.[128]

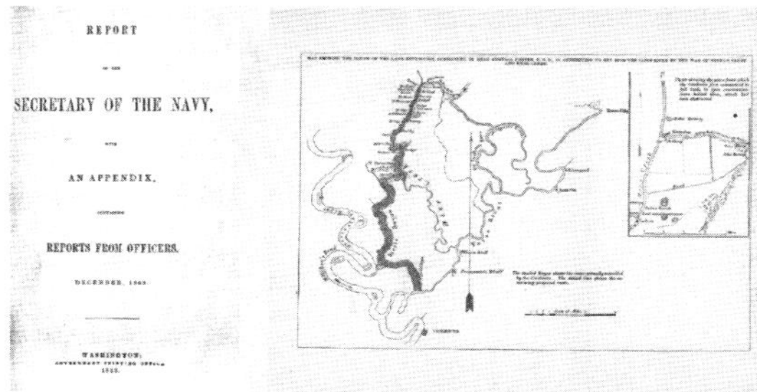

Steele's Bayou Expedition battle map. *Courtesy the Library of Congress.*

Federal troops having a hard time on the Steele's Bayou Expedition. *Courtesy the Library of Congress.*

For a time, as Porter ascended the creek, his decision made more and more sense. The farther they went, the wider and easier it got, but there was another problem. News of Porter's flotilla preceded it and soon reached the ears of Brigadier General Samuel Ferguson, Confederate cavalry commander charged with protecting the waterways north of Vicksburg. He immediately ordered his men to obstruct the rivers at Rolling Fork, blocking the Federals' pass into Big Sunflower River. He also sent for reinforcements.

By March 20, all five of Porter's ironclads had made it to Rolling Fork, where they were slowed by the Confederate obstructions. Ferguson's men arrived that same day and tried to attack, but a Federal battery and the ironclads themselves kept them at bay. Throughout the night, Ferguson's troopers felled trees behind the Union flotilla, trapping the ships. This is when Porter gave up the idea of pressing onward and focused all his energy into trying to escape. Fortunately for him, by the dawn of this date, the Rebels seemed unconcerned about capturing the ships. Sherman's men were nowhere to be seen, and he repeatedly sent requests for help. Of course, if Porter had not been so anxious to leave, Sherman's men wouldn't have

Major General Dabney Maury. *Courtesy the Library of Congress.*

had to catch up. Porter ordered his ships to back out of Rolling Fork and into Deer Creek. His men cleared the felled trees and debris as they went, while others prepared the ships to be scuttled if necessary to prevent the ships from falling into enemy hands.

Meanwhile, messages had reached Sherman of Porter's predicament, and he began to press his men forward and across Deer Creek as quickly as possible. As they went, they rounded up slaves so that Ferguson's men couldn't force them into cutting down more trees.

Meanwhile, Porter's retreat turned into a series of running skirmishes as Ferguson's men kept a respectful distance. Along the way, Federal troops and sailors set fire to pretty much anything they could—houses, plantations, fields, crops, all put to the torch to be kept out of Rebel hands. By late in the evening on March 21, the retreating flotilla and Sherman's men were close enough that the immediate danger was gone. It had been a hard, nearly impossible, march for both sides. The roads were mostly flooded, some under hip-high water, which is probably the reason Ferguson did not make any serious attempt to capture the ironclads—losing a golden opportunity that could have altered things to come. Regardless, the expedition fizzled out, and Porter's flotilla had returned to its starting point by March 24.[129]

Between March 23 and April 2, very little offensive operations were taking place by Quinby, and the Confederates seized the opportunity to go on the offensive. Loring noticed that the enemy was constructing a very heavy battery about one thousand yards from the fort. From April 2, and continuing through April 4, Loring ordered Confederate guns to shell the workers constructing the battery and sent sharpshooters to harass them. Major General Dabney Maury was ordered to carry out a forced reconnaissance on the left and right flanks. Maury reported that workmen were so annoyed by his sharpshooters that they were compelled to cease work before the battery was finished. During this time, the enemy was very quiet and sent no scouts out. Only one reconnaissance was made, with no reply to the firing of the guns or sharpshooters.[130]

This prompted Loring to report to Pemberton, "While our fire was destructive to their overcrowded camps, our action from right to left alarmed them very much, and on the night of April 4, they commenced embarking, and by daylight they were in rapid retreat up the river."[131] With this, the Federal fleet retired. Now all that was left to do was to go back up the river one hundred miles, *in reverse*, and explain to General Grant how ten thousand men and seven warships got licked by a fort made of cotton.

After conducting reconnaissance for twelve days and lacking small boats or pontoons to bypass Fort Pemberton, Quinby agreed that further attempts to take the position were futile. Even Wilson agreed that it was time to depart. This decision was reinforced when Confederate generals Maury and Tilghman found a way to attack the Federal headquarters. Maury stated in his memoirs that Brigadier General Lloyd Tilghman "proposed that we should try and break up the enemy's headquarters about a mile away from our front. Tilghman had been a civil engineer, and he had a county map showing the position of the farm-house where Quinby had his headquarters. He [Tilghman] trained his guns by the compass, while I sent in a body of sharp shooters through the woods on the enemy's right. We opened at the signal, and broke up the whole establishment, which retreated hastily for the Mississippi by way of the Yazoo [Pass]."[132]

A detachment of two hundred soldiers under Lieutenant Colonel Barnard Timmons was sent to reconnoiter the Federal camp. Upon arrival, the men discovered the Yankee fortifications and camp deserted. Fifteen graves were found. One of them was the chief gunner of the gunboat *Chillicothe*. More encouraging to the morale of the Rebels within Fort Pemberton were letters found from Federal soldiers despairing of ever taking "Fort Greenbush," the Federal name for the Rebel fort. In addition to the letters, it was reported that Timmon's forces captured "bacon and crackers by the quantity."[133]

In a letter to General Halleck, Grant wrote that he had ordered the withdrawal because of information he had received that "other and greater difficulties would be found in navigating the Yazoo below Greenwood." Men crowded the decks of the surviving transports and gunboats for the trip upriver. Officers received cabins, but enlisted men had to fend for themselves. Fires were not permitted to cook or keep warm, and the elements beat down on them as they slowly made their voyage back to the Mississippi.[134]

As the Federal flotilla made its retreat back up the river, Loring stated that the "overflow of the Tallahatchie and Coldwater Rivers made it impossible to get to the rivers except in small canoes." It was during this time that Captain George W. Mott of McCulloch's Cavalry ordered canoes made for the purpose of following and harassing the retreating enemy. Mott's company made contact with the flotilla and fired small arms and three rounds from a field piece into a "transport loaded with troops and doing considerable execution."[135]

All indications were that Quinby was in full retreat back to Helena, Arkansas. On April 4, Dabney sent Colonel O.S. Holland, in command of a regiment and a battalion of sharpshooters, with orders to discover the force and position of the enemy. Quinby formed a battle line to receive Holland's attack but was forced to retreat. By April 7, the flotilla had entered the Coldwater River. Dabney reported, "The operations of the enemy were characterized by a great want of energy, but by the usual disregard of the claims of humanity and of the usages of manly warfare; women and unarmed, helpless men were insulted, private dwellings and plantations were destroyed and plundered, the stock stolen or wantonly killed, the fruit trees belted, and every other means taken to gratify the cowardly instincts of base natures."[136]

By April 8, the entire force had cleared the Yazoo Pass. A soldier from the 33rd Missouri expressed his disappointment by saying, "I think we could have taken the fort any day we were there if our Generals had had made the attempt….None of us had the remotest idea of abandoning operations in front of the rebel fort and returning to Helena."[137]

An officer from the 72nd Illinois expressed a different view: "We are all sadly disappointed at not having a chance to take Fort Pemberton, but our generals are much more sensible than we are. They know that we can't take the fort, as it is impossible to bring a sufficient number of troops to operate at once as the fort is almost entirely surrounded by water….Lieutenant Colonel Wilson of General Grant's staff is here and sees for himself the impossibility of success and the utter uselessness of shedding blood where it would avail nothing."[138]

After receiving his final report on the expedition, Grant looked again at his map and chewed on his cigar, thinking about his next move to take Vicksburg. "This enterprise promised most fairly," he said, "but for some cause our troops and boats delayed so as to give the enemy time to fortify. My last information from this command was to the 17th (March). They were at Greenwood, on the Yazoo, a fortified place, and had abandoned all idea of getting past until they could receive additional ordnance stores. By a prompt movement Yazoo City could have been captured without opposition."[139]

"By daylight," reported General Loring of this date, "they were in rapid retreat up the river. We can hear of them steaming toward the Pass. How far they have got we are not fully advised, but think that they will go entirely through to the Mississippi."[140] He was right. Fort Pemberton was saved. The back door to Vicksburg was still closed, forcing Grant to renew his plans for the new campaign.

The Aftermath

Politically, the Yazoo Pass Expedition was viewed as a disaster for the Lincoln administration. Many believed that Grant should be removed. Abraham Lincoln responded to these critics, "I rather like the man. I think I will try him a little longer."[141] Eventually, this would develop into one of history's greatest military relationships between a president and his general.

The economic impact of the Yazoo Pass Expedition on the Mississippi Delta was very significant. Thousands of acres of crops were flooded by the breach in the levee, reducing the harvest in one of the most productive regions of the country and robbing the Confederacy of materials and foodstuffs. Federal forces confiscated and destroyed other staples, such as cotton. Mississippi Squadron vessels returned with 558 bales on their decks, and Federal reports indicate that approximately 4,000 to 5,000 bales of cotton were captured or destroyed, a retail loss of approximately $1.2 million to $1.5 million.[142]

The Yazoo Pass Expedition did not have an immediate military impact on the outcome of the war since neither side accomplished any strategic objectives. It did, however, delay the outcome of the Vicksburg Campaign.

The expedition forced Pemberton to react to Grant's maneuver and kept Confederate forces occupied near Fort Pemberton for nearly two weeks after the expedition departed, thus preventing Pemberton from concentrating his forces, allowing Grant time to develop his campaign plan for a final drive against Vicksburg.

Grant's decision to cancel the Yazoo Pass Expedition was based on available information that indicated the expedition had been stopped at Fort Pemberton. Efforts to conduct a supporting attack through Steele's Bayou, Black Bayou, Deer Creek and Rolling Fork failed. Water levels on the rivers were dropping, and the Yazoo Pass would be unusable in a few weeks. Lower water levels also provided the Confederates with opportunities to interdict the return route. Other courses of action, such as the efforts to bypass Vicksburg using canals, were not feasible. Grant needed to concentrate all of his forces, as well as Porter's gunboats, near Milliken's Bend to set the conditions for his next move.[143]

The Yazoo Pass Expedition, combined with other efforts, resulted in Confederate indecision. Pemberton was kept guessing as to Grant's true plans for approaching Vicksburg, forcing the Confederates to disperse their forces in case the route would be tried again. Colonel Waul and his Texas Legion remained at Fort Pemberton to supervise improvements and recommended to Pemberton on April 27 that the fortifications remain in place until mid-May. He justified this action by explaining that falling river levels, combined with Federal troop dispositions, would make another attack down the Tallahatchie unlikely after another two weeks.[144]

For Confederate general Loring, the past few months had been filled with dismay and consternation as he watched more and more Federal reinforcements appear before him at Fort Pemberton. He and his band of Rebels had driven off two Federal ironclads several times before the Federals retreated. Loring was, of course, thrilled at first, basking in the triumph of his own success. In the meantime, Grant allowed the Confederates to have their victory; this distracted them from his true plans, soon going into effect, that ultimately would lead to the fall of Vicksburg.

Order of Battle

Yazoo Pass Campaign, February 3–April 10, 1863

Union Forces

Commanding Expedition

Brig. Gen. Leonard F. Ross (February 15–March 21, 1863)
Brig. Gen. Isaac Quinby (March 21–April 10, 1863)

13th Division, Brig. Gen. Leonard F. Ross
- 1st Brigade, Brig. Gen. Frederick Salamon
  - 43rd Indiana Infantry
  - 46th Indiana Infantry
  - 47th Indiana Infantry
- 2nd Brigade, Brig. Gen. Clinton B. Fisk
  - 29th Iowa Infantry
  - 33rd Iowa Infantry
  - 36th Iowa Infantry
  - 33rd Missouri Infantry
  - 28th Wisconsin Infantry

Artillery
Company A, 1st Missouri Artillery (6 guns)
3rd Battery, Iowa Light Artillery (6 guns)
7th Division, Brig. Gen. Isaac Quinby
1st Brigade, Col. John B. Sanborn
72nd Illinois Infantry
48th Indiana Infantry
59th Indiana Infantry
4th Minnesota Infantry
2nd Brigade, Col. Charles L. Matthies
56th Illinois Infantry
17th Iowa Infantry
10th Missouri Infantry
24th Missouri Infantry, Company F
80th Ohio Infantry
3rd Brigade, Col. George B. Boomer
93rd Illinois Infantry
5th Iowa Infantry
10th Iowa Infantry
26th Missouri Infantry
Artillery
1st Missouri Artillery, Company M (6 guns)
11th Battery, Ohio Light Artillery (6 guns)
6th Battery, Wisconsin Light Artillery (6 guns)
12th Battery, Wisconsin Artillery (6 guns)
Cavalry
2nd Illinois Cavalry, Company E
5th Missouri Cavalry, Company C

Unattached
1st Indiana Cavalry
24th Indiana Infantry
34th Indiana Infantry

Union Naval Flotilla

COMMANDING GUNBOATS
LCDR Watson Smith (Medically Surveyed)
LCDR James P. Foster
Iron Clads: *Baron De Kalb*, *Chillicothe*
Tinclads: *Rattler*, *Marmora*, *Signal*, *Romeo*, *Petrel*, *Forest Rose*
Rams: *Dick Fulton*, *Liones*

CONFEDERATE FORCES

Commanding Confederate Forces

MAJ. GEN. W.W. LORING

1st Brigade, Brig. Gen. Lloyd Tilghman
54th Alabama Infantry
8th Kentucky Infantry
20th Mississippi Infantry
23rd Mississippi Infantry
26th Mississippi Infantry
14th Mississippi Artillery Battalion, Company C (4 guns)

2nd Brigade, Brig. Gen. Winfield S. Featherston
3rd Mississippi Infantry
22nd Mississippi Infantry
31st Mississippi Infantry
33rd Mississippi Infantry
1st Mississippi Sharpshooters Battalion
1st Mississippi Light Artillery, Company C (4 guns)

Moore's Brigade, Brig. Gen. John C. Moore
37th Alabama Infantry
42nd Alabama Infantry
35th Mississippi Infantry
40th Mississippi Infantry

2nd Texas Infantry
Bledsoe's Missouri Battery (4 guns)

3rd Brigade, Mississippi State Troops, Brig. Gen. J.Z. George

Not Brigaded
37th Mississippi Infantry
7th Tennessee Infantry
Waul's Texas Legion
Company B, Pointe Coupee Artillery (4 guns)
Company A, Pointe Coupee Artillery (4 guns)
Tobbins Tennessee Artillery (4 guns)
Detachment, 21st Louisiana Infantry
Company A, 22nd Louisiana Infantry
Naval detachment commanded by Lt. F.E. Sheppard
2nd Missouri Cavalry
2nd Arkansas Cavalry
Blythe's Battalion, Mississippi State Troops

Notes

Chapter 1

1. NavSource Online, "CSS St. Philip"; *Post and Courier*, "Charleston at War."
2. *New York Times*, "Capt. McGowan's Report."
3. Miller, "Elegant, Luxurious Star of the West," 8.
4. Channing, *Crisis of Fear*, 230; Redding, "Voices of Secession."
5. Catton, *Coming Fury*, 176–81; Swanberg, *First Blood*, 144–49; *Official Records of the Union and Confederate Navies*, ser. 1, vol. 4, 220–23 (hereafter *ORN*); *New York Herald*, "Secret Movements of United States Troops"; *New York Times*, "Capt. McGowan's Report."
6. Cooper, *Traitors*, 44–45. Major Anderson did not receive the letter until the morning of January 9, 1861, after the *Star of the West* was fired on. Governor Pickens had authorized the delivery of mail to the Federal troops in Fort Sumter.
7. *New York Times*, "Capt. McGowan's Report."
8. *Harper's Weekly*, "Firing on the Star of the West," 54. This issue of *Harper's Weekly* includes the eyewitness account of a reporter on board the *Star of the West* that day, along with the eyewitness account of John McGowan, captain of the steamship.
9. Baker, *Cadets in Gray*, 18–19; George Edward Haynsworth (1841–1887), Citadel class of 1861, served as a lieutenant in the 1st Regiment South Carolina Artillery. He survived the war and became a schoolteacher, a

lawyer and a judge; *Harper's Weekly*, "Firing on the Star of the West," 54. An illustration on page 52 of this edition of *Harper's Weekly* depicts the Morris Island battery firing on the *Star of the West*.

10. Samuel Bonneau Pickens (1839–1892), Citadel class of 1862, attained the rank of colonel in the 12th Alabama Regiment. He survived the war and became an agent for the Charleston Railroad. Thomas B. Ferguson (1841–1922), Citadel class of 1861, attained the rank of major in Walker's Division of Johnston's Army. Although seriously wounded in Mississippi, he recovered to command the First Military District. He survived the war and became a U.S. diplomat; Baker, *Cadets in Gray*, 19.
11. *New York Times*, "Capt. McGowan's Report"; *Harper's Weekly*, "Firing on the Star of the West," 54.
12. *Charleston Mercury*, "Ninth of January"; "War Begun. Engagement at Fort Morris."
13. *New York Times*, "Capt. McGowan's Report"; *Harper's Weekly*, "Firing on the Star of the West," 54.
14. *Post and Courier*, "Charleston at War"; *New York Times*, "Capt. McGowan's Report."
15. *Richmond Dispatch*, "National Crisis"; Meerse, "Buchanan, Corruption, and the Election of 1860," 12; Holt, "James Buchanan, 1857–1861," 86–96; *Charleston Mercury*, "Progress of Secession"; *Harper's Weekly*, "Firing on the Star of the West"; *Charleston Mercury*, "War Begun."
16. *Harper's Weekly*, January 19, 1861.
17. *Richmond Daily Dispatch*, "Engagement at Charleston."
18. *Charleston Mercury*, "Alabama Is Out of the Union"; Davis, *Government of Our Own*, 12, 120, 127, 224–25.
19. *Official Records of the Union and Confederate Armies*, ser. 1, vol. 1, 624–25 (hereafter *OR*).
20. *New York Times*, "Star of the West Seizure"; Sprague, *Treachery in Texas*, 136.
21. Fraiser, *Mississippi River Country Tales*, 80.
22. Posey, "Capture of the Star of the West," 74; *ORN*, ser. 1, vol. 16, 534, 572; Miller, "Elegant, Luxurious Star of the West."
23. *ORN*, ser. 1, vol. 18, 350; vol. 19, 137; *OR*, vol. 24, pt. 1, 415; Holmes, "End of the 'Star of the West.'" The grave of Lieutenant A.A. Stoddard is marked by a Confederate headstone at the Old Greenwood City Cemetery in Greenwood, Mississippi.

CHAPTER 2

24. *OR*, ser. 1, vol. 51, pt. 1, 370.
25. Elliot, *Winfield Scott*, 698; *OR*, ser. 1, vol. 51, pt. 1, 387.
26. *OR*, ser. 1, vol. 51, pt. 1, 387.
27. Porter, *Incidents and Anecdotes*, 95–96.
28. Gabel, *Vicksburg Campaign*, 7–8.
29. Porter, *Naval History of the Civil War*, 268.
30. McFeely, *Grant, a Biography*, 48–49, 65–66.
31. Bands, *Man Who Saved the Union*, 151, 164–65, 188–89, 191, 211–12; Flood, *Grant and Sherman*, 71, 109, 112, 114, 133, 143–44; McFeely, *Grant, a Biography*, 92–94, 114; Smith, *Grant*, 111, 125–34, 138–64, 225–27; Bonekemper, *Grant and Lee*, 51, 53, 58–59, 63–64, 94; Longacre, *General Ulysses S. Grant*, 137.
32. Catton, *Grant Moves South*, 371–72.
33. Bands, *Man Who Saved the Union*, 124–25; Flood, *Grant and Sherman*, 147–48.
34. Smith, *Fight for the Yazoo*, 76.
35. Ibid.
36. *OR*, ser. 1, vol. 15, 820; vol. 17, 717, 726–27.
37. *OR*, vol. 24, pt. 3, 611.
38. Sides, "Civil War in North Mississippi."
39. Simon, *Papers of Ulysses S. Grant*, 7:44.
40. Dill and McClanahan, "Battle of Coffeeville."
41. *OR*, ser. 1, vol. 17, pt. 1, 471–74, 503–7.
42. Ibid., 475; Grant, *Personal Memoirs*, 228.
43. The National Park Service battle description gives an alternative name, Chickasaw Bluffs. Although this may be derived from a variation on "Bluffs over Chickasaw Bayou" (referring to Drumgould's Bluff), the geographic location known as Chickasaw Bluffs is distant from the battlefield. Other references to this article do not use this name.
44. Eicher, *Longest Night*, 30; Bearss, *Campaign for Vicksburg*, 224–26; Kennedy, *Civil War Battlefield Guide*, 156; Ballard, *Vicksburg*, 131–33.
45. Ballard, *Vicksburg*, 144; Bearss, *Campaign for Vicksburg*, 211; Ambrose, "Struggle for Vicksburg," 4–66.
46. *OR*, ser. 1, vol. 17, 613.

CHAPTER 3

47. *OR*, ser. 1, vol. 2, 641.
48. West, "Gunboats in the Swamps," 157.
49. Winters, *Music of the Mocking Birds*, 27–28; Boyd, *Civil War Diary of Cyrus F. Boyd*, 114; Foote, *Civil War*, 191.
50. Milligan, *Gunboats Down the Mississippi*, 130; Smith, *Fight for the Yazoo*, 20–39; Grant, *Memoirs and Selected Letters*, 297.
51. Taken from the National Park Service information on naval personnel during the Civil War on July 24, 2016, https://www.nps.gov/wicr/learn/historyculture/Navy-Personnel.htm.
52. *ORN*, vol. 23, 405; Smith, *Fight for the Yazoo*, 20–39; Grant, *Memoirs and Selected Letters*, 297; Catton, "Bluecoats in the Bayous," 34.
53. Shea and Winschel, *Vicksburg Is the Key*, 69; *OR*, ser. 1, vol. 24, pt. 1, 376.
54. *OR*, ser. 1, vol. 24, pt. 1, 249–50; Bearss, *Campaign for Vicksburg*, 482–83.
55. Smith, *Fight for the Yazoo*, 2.
56. Shea and Winschel, *Vicksburg Is the Key*, 68–69; *ORN*, ser. 1, vol. 24, 258, notes that the date of building the levee was 1853.
57. Grant, *Personal Memoirs of U.S. Grant*, 266; *OR*, ser. 1, vol. 24, pt. 1, 10.
58. *OR*, ser. 1, vol. 24, pt. 1, 371–72.
59. Carter, *Final Fortress*, 135.
60. Bearss, *Decision in Mississippi*, 149–80; *OR*, ser. 1, vol. 24, pt. 1, 373.
61. *OR*, ser. 1, vol. 24, pt. 1, 374–75.
62. *ORN*, ser. 1, vol. 24, 251.
63. *OR*, ser. 1, vol. 24, pt. 1, 377–78; pt. 3, 622; Smith, *Fight for the Yazoo*, 181. I have not been able to prove the wild pig encounter with Captain Forrest since there seems to be no report about his encounter with the pigs. The only account of this incident comes from Captain Brown, written many years after the war and recorded as a footnote in Ed Bearss's Vicksburg Campaign trilogy, volume 1, 490. The account was related to Brown by General Cadwallader C. Washburn, who probably got the story from captured Confederate soldiers. In December, Washburn had commanded the failed Union expedition to Grenada, ending with the Battle of Oakland.
64. *ORN*, vol. 24, 163.
65. Ibid., 251.
66. Ibid.
67. Ibid., 252.
68. *OR*, vol. 24, pt. 3, 54; Grant's reference to "General Ross" is to Brigadier General Benjamin L. Ross.

69. Warner, *Generals in Blue*, 411–12.
70. *OR*, ser. 1, vol. 24, pt. 1, 374–75; Shea and Winschel, *Vicksburg Is the Key*, 70; Catton, "Bluecoats in the Bayous," 34.
71. Bearss, *Campaign for Vicksburg*, 537.
72. 28th Wisconsin Volunteer Infantry, "Service and Engagements."
73. *New York Herald*, "Yazoo Pass Expedition."
74. *OR*, ser. 1, vol. 24, pt. 1, 377–78.
75. Heidler and Heidler, "Major General William Wing Loring."
76. *OR*, vol. 24, pt. 3, 623.

CHAPTER 4

77. *New York Herald*, "Yazoo Pass Expedition."
78. *ORN*, vol. 24, 294.
79. *OR*, ser. 1, vol. 24, pt. 1, 630–33.
80. Ibid., pt. 2, 641.
81. Gillespie, "Fort Pemberton," 4–5.
82. Hasskarl, *Waul's Texas Legion*, 15.
83. National Register of Historic Places Inventory, Nomination Form, "Fort Pemberton." The owner of the property is U.S. Corps of Engineers in the Vicksburg District. The location of legal description is in the Chancery Clerk's Office of the Leflore County Courthouse in Greenwood, Mississippi; *OR*, ser. 1, vol. 24, pt. 1, 415.
84. *OR*, ser. 1, vol. 24, pt. 3, 638–39.
85. Hewett, *Supplement to the Official Records*, 69:76–112; Raab, *W.W. Loring*, 63.
86. *OR*, ser. 1, vol. 24, pt. 1, 394; vol. 17, pt. 1, 253. The twenty-pounder in reference here is the "Lady Richardson," captured from Corinth, Mississippi. The three-inch rifled light cannon was nicknamed the "Lady Polk," a Blakely cannon made in England and shipped through the blockade. The "Lady Polk" has been restored to firing condition and is on display at the Museum of the Mississippi Delta in Greenwood, Mississippi. The cannon is occasionally taken out by local reenactors and fired at Fort Pemberton Park.
87. *ORN*, vol. 24, 296. The *Star of the West* and other vessels were moved from New Orleans to Yazoo City, Mississippi, after it fell to Farragut in the spring of 1862.
88. Ibid.
89. Ibid., 296–97, 448.

90. *OR*, ser. 1, vol. 24, pt. 3, 665–66.
91. Ibid., 86–87.
92. Ibid., pt. 1, 406.
93. *New York Herald*, "Yazoo Pass Expedition."
94. *ORN*, vol. 24, 296.
95. *OR*, ser. 1, vol. 24, pt. 1, 394.
96. Ibid., 399.
97. Ibid., 380.
98. *New York Herald*, "Yazoo Pass Expedition."
99. *ORN*, ser. 1, vol. 24, 246, 284, 299, 541, 693; Dooley, *Joint Operations*, 56; *New York Herald*, "Yazoo Pass Expedition."
100. *ORN*, ser. 1, vol. 24, 246.
101. *OR*, ser. 1, vol. 24, pt. 1, 379, 395, 397, 401, 412; pt. 3, 21; *ORN*, vol. 24, 247.
102. *OR*, ser. 1, vol. 24, pt. 1, 379, 395, 397, 401, 412; pt. 3, 21; *ORN*, vol. 24, 247.
103. *OR*, ser. 1, vol. 24, pt. 1, 379, 395, 397, 401, 412; pt. 3, 21; *ORN*, vol. 24, 247.

Chapter 5

104. Eicher, *Longest Night*, 440. Allegedly, General William W. Loring earned his nickname "Old Blizzards" when he was heard to shout out, "Give them blizzards!" as he encouraged his artillery to keep up their rate of fire on the Union fleet at Fort Pemberton.
105. *New York Herald*, "Yazoo Pass Expedition."
106. 28th Wisconsin Volunteer Infantry, "2nd Lieutenant Lauren Baker."
107. *OR*, ser. 1, vol. 24, 280.
108. Ibid., pt. 3, 663.
109. *ORN*, vol. 24, 268–73; *OR*, ser. 1, vol. 24, pt. 1, 295.
110. Sperry, *History of the 33d Iowa Infantry*, 19–20.
111. *OR*, ser. 1, vol. 24, pt. 1, 379, 395, 397, 401, 412; pt. 3, 21; *ORN*, vol. 24, 247.
112. *OR*, ser. 1, vol. 24, pt. 1, 379, 395, 397, 401, 412; pt. 3, 21; *ORN*, ser. 1, vol. 24, 273.
113. *OR*, ser. 1, vol. 24, pt. 1, 395, 397; *ORN*, ser. 1, vol. 24, 273–75.
114. 28th Wisconsin Volunteer Infantry, "2nd Lieutenant Lauren Baker."
115. See 28th Wisconsin Volunteer Infantry website about an eyewitness report on the raid of McNutt, Mississippi. Reported by Corporal Charles H. Wildish of Company A, 28th Wisconsin Volunteer Infantry.

116. 28th Wisconsin Volunteer Infantry, "2nd Lieutenant Lauren Baker"; Hemphill, *Fevers, Floods and Faith*, 101. Legend has it that that the county treasurer took county funds and placed them in saddlebags to be buried at an undisclosed location in the area. Upon his capture by the Federal troops and discovery of the county treasury missing, he was questioned, tortured and shot without revealing the treasury's location. Many people believe that it's hidden at McNutt Cemetery, which survived the town after the war and is still in use today. The legend draws many treasure seekers every year.
117. *OR*, ser. 1, vol. 24, pt. 1, 412–13, 416.
118. Ibid., 416.
119. Ibid., 412–13.
120. *ORN*, ser. 1, vol. 24, 280–84; *OR*, ser. 1, vol. 24, pt. 1, 414–15; pt. 3, 672, 682.
121. *ORN*, ser. 1, vol. 24, 286; Hasskarl, *Waul's Texas Legion*, 16; Johnson and Buell, *Battles and Leaders of the Civil War*, 3:561.
122. *ORN*, ser. 1, vol. 24, 280–84.
123. Ibid., 255, 287; *OR*, ser. 1, vol. 24, pt. 1, 419; pt. 3, 693.
124. *New York Times*, "Siege of Vicksburg."
125. *OR*, ser. 1, vol. 24, pt. 1, 419–21; *ORN*, ser. 1, vol. 24, 283.
126. *ORN*, vol. 24, 474.
127. Ibid., 480.
128. *OR*, ser. 1, vol. 24, pt. 1, 396–98, 413–14.
129. Bearss, *Vicksburg Campaign*, 479–595. The Yazoo Pass and Steele's Bayou Expedition are discussed; *ORN*, ser. 1, vol. 23, 709; ser. 1, vol. 24, 294.
130. *OR*, ser. 1, vol. 24, pt. 1, 420.
131. Ibid., 419–20.
132. Maury, *Recollections of a Virginian*, 177–78.
133. Waul's Texas Legion SCV Camp 2103, "Diary of Edwin E. Rice." Interestingly enough, Captain Wickeland's Company K had a high percentage of German-born immigrants from Austin County. Three of the members of the offending company were brothers, all named Franke, the author's great-grandfather and great-uncles.
134. *ORN*, vol. 24, 289–91; Shea and Winschel, *Vicksburg Is the Key*, 72.
135. *OR*, ser. 1, vol. 24, pt. 1, 419–20.
136. Ibid.
137. Unpublished letters of Henry S. Carroll.
138. Stockton, *War Diary*, 11.
139. *OR*, ser. 1, vol. 15, 300.
140. *OR*, ser. 1, vol. 25, pt. 1, 151.

THE AFTERMATH

141. Merrill, *Soldier of Indiana*, 293–94.
142. *ORN*, vol. 24, 284, 541–44.
143. Ibid., 537, 544–45; 501–11.
144. Hasskarl, *Waul's Texas Legion*, 21.

SELECTED BIBLIOGRAPHY

PRIMARY SOURCES

Boyd, Cyrus F. *The Civil War Diary of Cyrus F. Boyd, Fifteenth Iowa Infantry, 1861–1863*. Edited by Mildred Throne. Baton Rouge: Louisiana State University Press, 1998.

Grant, Ulysses S. *Memoirs and Selected Letters: Personal Memoirs of U.S. Grant, Selected Letters, 1839–1865*. New York: Library of America, 1990.

———. *Personal Memoirs.* New York: Da Capo Press, 1982.

———. *Personal Memoirs of U.S. Grant*. N.p.: Create Space Independent Publishing Platform, 2013.

Johnson, Robert Underwood, and Clarence Clough Buell. *Battles and Leaders of the Civil War*. Vol. 3. N.p.: Century Company, 1888.

Porter, David Dixon. *Incidents and Anecdotes of the Civil War.* New York, 1885.

———. *The Naval History of the Civil War*. New York: Sherman Publishing, 1886.

Simon, John Y., ed. *The Papers of Ulysses S. Grant.* 22 vols. Carbondale: Southern Illinois University Press, 1967.

Sperry, A.F. *History of the 33d Iowa Infantry Volunteer Regiment, 1863–66*. Des Moines, IA: Mills and Company, 1866.

Sprague, J.T. *The Treachery in Texas: The Secession of Texas and the Arrest of United States Officers and Soldiers Serving in Texas*. New York: printed for the New York Historical Society, 1862.

Stockton, Joseph. *War Diary of Brevet Brigadier General Joseph Stockton*. Gregory Coco Papers, Harrisburg Civil War Roundtable Collection, U.S. Army Military History Institute, Carlisle, PA.

Winters, William. *The Music of the Mocking Birds, the Roar of the Cannon: The Civil War Diary and Letters of William Winters*. Edited by Steven E. Woodworth. Lincoln: University of Nebraska Press, 1998.

Published Records of the United States Government

Gabel, Charles R. *The Vicksburg Campaign, November 1862–July 1863*. Washington, D.C.: Center of Military History United States Army, 2013.

Official Records of the Union and Confederate Armies During the War of Rebellion. Washington, D.C.: Government Printing Office, 1886.

Official Records of the Union and Confederate Navies During the War of Rebellion. Washington, D.C.: Government Printing Office, 1896.

Primary Newspaper and Magazine Articles

Charleston Mercury. "Alabama Is Out of the Union." January 12, 1861.

———. "The Ninth of January." January 10, 1861.

———. "The Progress of Secession." December 31, 1860.

———. "The War Begun." January 10, 1861.

———. "War Begun. Engagement at Fort Morris." January 10, 1861.

Dill, Benjamin, and John R. McClanahan. "Battle of Coffeeville." *Memphis Appeal*, December 13, 1862.

Harper's Weekly. "The Firing on the Star of the West" (January 26, 1861): 54.

———. "Governor Pickens of South Carolina" (January 19, 1861).

New York Herald. "Secret Movements of United States Troops." January 8, 1861.

———. "The Yazoo Pass Expedition." March 25, 1863.

New York Times. "Capt. McGowan's Report; Steamship Star of the West." January 14, 1861.

———. "The Siege of Vicksburg; The Yazoo Pass Expedition Still in Front of Fort Pemberton; Gunboat Reconnaissance of Haines' Bluff; Two Important Expeditions Under Way." April 8, 1863.

———. "The Star of the West Seizure; How It Was Done; Arrival of the Officers; Impressment of the Crew." May 2, 1861.

Posey, Mrs. Samuel. "Capture of the Star of the West." *Confederate Veteran* 32, no. 74.

Richmond Daily Dispatch. "The Engagement at Charleston." January 12, 1861.

Richmond Dispatch. "The National Crisis." December 31, 1860.

Unpublished Letters

Gillespie, W.A. "Fort Pemberton." A letter to the J.Z. George Chapter United Daughters of the Confederacy, Greenwood, Mississippi, May 3, 1904.

Henry S. Carroll Collection. The unpublished letters of Henry S. Carroll. Carlisle Barracks, PA: Military History Institute Archives, 1863.

SECONDARY SOURCES

Baker, Gary R. *Cadets in Gray*. Lexington, SC: Palmetto Bookworks, 1989.

Ballard, Michael B. *Vicksburg: The Campaign that Opened the Mississippi*. Chapel Hill: University of North Carolina Press, 2004.

Bands, H.W. *The Man Who Saved the Union: Ulysses S. Grant in War and Peace*. New York: Doubleday, 2012.

Bearss, Edwin C. *The Campaign for Vicksburg*. Vol. 1, *Vicksburg Is the Key*. Dayton, OH: Morningside House, 1985.

———. *Decision in Mississippi.* Jackson: Mississippi Commission on the War Between the States, 1962.

Bonekemper, Edward H., III *Grant and Lee*. Washington, D.C.: Regnery History, 2012.

Carter, Samuel. *The Final Fortress: The Campaign for Vicksburg, 1862–1863*. New York: St. Martin's Press, 1980.

Catton, Bruce. *The Coming Fury.* New York: Doubleday and Company, 1961.

———. *Grant Moves South.* New York: Little, Brown and Company Inc., 1960.

Channing, Steven A. *Crisis of Fear: Secession in South Carolina*. New York: Simon and Schuster, 1970.

Cooper, Edward S. *Traitors: The Secession Period, November 1860–July 1861*. N.p.: Rosemont Publishing and Printing, 2008.

Davis, William C. *A Government of Our Own*. New York: Free Press, 1994.

Dooley, Colonel Michael J. *Joint Operations During the Vicksburg Campaign of 1863: The Yazoo Pass Expedition*. Carlisle Barracks, PA: U.S. Army War College, 2000.

Eicher, David J. *The Longest Night: A Military History of the Civil War*. New York: Simon & Schuster, 2001.

Elliot, Charles Winslow. *Winfield Scott: The Soldier and the Man*. New York, 1937.

Flood, Charles Bracelen. *Grant and Sherman: The Friendship that Won the Civil War.* New York: Harper Perennial, 2006.

Foote, Shelby. *The Civil War, a Narrative: Fredericksburg to Meridian*. New York: Random House, 1963.

Fraiser, Jim. *Mississippi River Country Tales: A Celebration of 500 Years of Deep South History*. Gretna, LA: Pelican Publishing, 2001.

Hasskarl, Robert A. *Waul's Texas Legion, 1862–1865*. Madison: University of Wisconsin–Madison, Book Bindery, 1976.

Hemphill, Marie H. *Fevers, Floods and Faith: A History of Sunflower County, 1844–1876*. Indianola, MS: Marie H. Hemphill, 1980.

Hewett, Janet B., ed. *Supplement to the Official Records of the Union and Confederate Armies*. Vol. 69. Wilmington, NC: Broadfoot Publishing Company, 1996.

Holt, Michael F. "James Buchanan, 1857–1861." In *Response of the Presidents to Charges of Misconduct*. Edited by C. Vann Woodward. New York, 1974.

Kennedy, Frances H., ed. *The Civil War Battlefield Guide*. 2nd ed. Boston: Houghton Mifflin Company, 1998.

Longacre, Edward G. *General Ulysses S. Grant: The Soldier and the Man*. Cambridge, MA: First Da Capo Press, 2006.

Maury, Dabney Herndon. *Recollections of a Virginian in the Mexican, Indian, and Civil Wars*. New York: Scribner's Sons, 1897.

McFeely, William F. *Grant, a Biography*. New York: W.W. Norton, 1981.

Merrill, Catherine. *The Soldier of Indiana in the War for the Union*. Indianapolis, IN: Merrill and Company, 1866–69.

Milligan, John D. *Gunboats Down the Mississippi*. North Stratford, NH: Ayer Company Publishers, 1980.

Raab, James W. *W.W. Loring: Florida's Forgotten General*. Manhattan, KS: Sunflower University Press, 1996.

Shea, William L., and Terrence J. Winschel. *Vicksburg Is the Key: The Struggle for the Mississippi River*. Lincoln: University of Nebraska, 2003.

Smith, Jean Edward. *Grant.* New York: Simon & Schuster, 2001.

Smith, Myron J., Jr. *The Fight for the Yazoo, August 1862–July 1864: Swamps, Forts, and Fleets on Vicksburg's Northern Flank*. Jefferson, NC: McFarland & Company, 2012.

Swanberg, W.A. *First Blood*. New York: Scribner, 1957.

Warner, Ezra J. *Generals in Blue: Lives of the Union Commanders*. Baton Rouge: Louisiana State University Press, 1964.

Articles

Ambrose, Stephen E. "Struggle for Vicksburg: The Battles and Siege that Decided the Civil War." *Civil War Times Illustrated* (July 1967): 4–66.

Catton, Bruce. "Bluecoats in the Bayous." *Boys Life Magazine* (May 1961): 34.

Holmes, Jack D.L. "The End of the 'Star of the West.'" *Civil War Times* (October 1961).

Meerse, David E. "Buchanan, Corruption, and the Election of 1860." *Civil War History* 12, no. 2 (June 1966): 12.

Miller, Dr. Mary C. "Elegant, Luxurious Star of the West Met a Decidedly Unromantic Fate in the Mississippi Delta." *America's Civil War* (November 1993): 8.

Post and Courier. "Charleston at War: The Star of the West Gets First Taste of the War." January 2, 2011.

Redding, Nicholas A. "Voices of Secession." *Hallowed Ground* (2010).

West, Richard S. "Gunboats in the Swamps: The Yazoo Pass Expedition." *Civil War History* 9, no. 2 (June 1963): 157.

Websites

Heidler, David, and Jeanne Heidler. "Major General William Wing Loring, C.S.A. (1818–1886)." This Week in the Civil War. August 1, 2011. http://thisweekinthecivilwar.com.

NavSource Online. "CSS St. Philip." May 14, 2016. http://www.navsource.org/archives/09/86/86496.htm.

Sides, Don. "The Civil War in North Mississippi, November/December, 1862." Mississippi Central Railroad Campaign. http://www.angelfire.com/ms2/grantshilohvicksburg.

28th Wisconsin Volunteer Infantry. "2nd Lieutenant Lauren Barker, Co. A." http://www.28thwisconsin.com/veterans/l_barker.html.

———. "Service and Engagements of the 28th Wisconsin Infantry." http://www.28thwisconsin.com/service/yazoo.html.

Waul's Texas Legion SCV Camp 2103. "Diary of Edwin E. Rice; April 15, 1862–April 5, 1863." Transcribed by David S. Pettus. http://www.waulstexaslegion.com/files/WTL_Diary.docx.

Index

V

W

Y

About the Author

Larry McCluney has been a member of the Sons of Confederate Veterans for twenty-five years. He currently serves as a national officer of the Sons of Confederate Veterans; is combined boards chairman of the nonprofit that oversees Beauvoir, Last Home of Confederate President Jefferson Davis; is a former member of the Golden Triangle Civil War Round Table; and is a Civil War Living Historian. He received his master's degree in history from Mississippi State University. Larry has taught history at the high school level in the Mississippi public school system for twenty-four years and is an instructor at Mississippi Delta Community College. He has won numerous awards from the United Daughters of the Confederacy and the Sons of Confederate Veterans for historical preservation. He lives in Greenwood, Mississippi, with his wife, Julia.